ANNI SENNO

BALANCE ON ALL LEVELS
WITH THE CRYSTAL AND INDIGO ENERGIES

good adventures publishing

Balance on All Levels with the Crystal and Indigo Energies
©2016, Anni Sennov and Good Adventures Publishing
First edition, second impression
Set with Cambria
Layout: Anni Sennov – www.good-adventures.dk
Cover design: Michael Bernth – www.monovoce.dk
Cover photo: Pata Degerman
Author photo: Lisbeth Hjort – www.lisbethhjort.dk

Original title(s) in Danish:
"Balance på alle planer" and
"Krystalbørn, Indigobørn & Fremtidens voksne"
Translated into English by: David Tugwell
Proofread by: Sue Jonas Dupuis

ISBN 978-87-92549-70-9

Acknowledgements

Many thanks to the Finn Pata Degerman for allowing me to use his beautiful photograph on the cover of this book. The picture was taken at Ekenäs' archipelago in southern Finland at midnight.

Notice

Although the author and publisher have made every effort to ensure the accuracy and completeness of information contained in this book, we assume no responsibility for errors, inaccuracies, omissions, or any inconsistency herein. Any offence caused to people, places, or organizations is unintentional.

Readers should use their own judgment or consult a holistic medical expert or their personal physician for specific applications to their individual problems.

Contents

Introduction

This book is a combined and updated version of my two books *"Balance on All Levels"* from 2002 and *"Crystal Children, Indigo Children and Adults of the Future"* from 2004.

This book tells you what an AuraTransformation™ is. It also describes the difference between the three aura structures – the old time soul aura, the New Time Indigo aura and Crystal aura. You are also shown how different areas of life – both personal and energetic – are each in their own way affected by an Aura-Transformation™.

There is also a discussion of the concepts of masculine and feminine, which are of great importance for the balancing which is always a follow-up to an AuraTransformation™. The latter part of the book will give you insight into the phenomenon of Aura-Transformation™ from a spiritual perspective.

If after reading this you are interested in having an AuraTransformation™, you can find a selection of qualified Aura Mediators at **www.auratransformation.com**.

I wish you the best of luck on your path and really hope that at some time you will choose the New Time aura with the opportunities it has to offer you, if it feels right for you to do so.

Best wishes

Anni Sennov
Spring 2011

The Story Behind AuraTransformation™

When I was very young, I had no idea that there was anything called the alternative world. I only knew about horoscopes in magazines, which I was very interested in – imagine being able to predict the future!

When I was 17 years old, I began to read about astrology, which became my all-consuming hobby and at the age of 22 I became acquainted with healing, meditation, planet journeys and regression therapy and my personal concept of the world really began to break down. So I decided to put aside this newly acquired knowledge of alternative lifestyles for the next few years.

When I was 27 I became seriously ill for three and a half years with very severe eczema. During this period I was given a whole range of treatments by members of the established medical system but with no tangible results. I also tried everything in the world of alternative therapies but nothing helped much for this very painful condition.

One hot summer's day I made up my mind that I would be healthy no matter what, and that the responsibility for being well in the future had to be my own and that I would stop constantly putting my life in the hands of different therapists. It was then that a 'miracle' took place.

In under two weeks my eczema was gone and I was also pregnant. These two things seemed to me to have arisen from my conscious choice to take responsibility for my own life.

However I was not yet aware that, unlike most other people, I had no energy bodies in my aura. Several years passed where I limited myself to horoscope reading and healing, as well as looking after my small son, before receiving the message that became AuraTransformation™ as the solution to my previous skin problem suddenly came through. It was at this point that things really started to take off in my healing practice. This provoked a great deal of resistance from the outside world. The people around me and a number of alternative practitioners clearly felt that I had a screw loose. How on earth was I able to pick up energy states which were so far beyond any previous channelled spiritual knowledge?

This can be explained by the fact that other people's auras were still intact whereas mine was not, due to the fact of my illness. Strangely enough this was not picked up by any of the psychics I visited during this period. They were unable to relate to energy states in me that were far beyond their own framework of understanding, something which still prevails in some spiritual circles to this day, although fortunately the understanding of energy is far more advanced these days.

There is no doubt that I must have seemed to be extremely provocative to many of my alternative therapy colleagues when I seriously began to work on spreading the concept of Aura-Transformation™.

Today, however, there are many trained Aura Mediators, particularly in Scandinavia, who, fortunately, are all able to speak about the concept in a more moderate way than I did when I made my breakthrough in 1996.

My own AuraTransformation™ came about with the help of a friend who was a healer and able to channel very powerful energies.

Before the healing, I had received some clear signals that I needed to integrate stronger protection around my body and that it should happen quickly because my aura was 'leaking' energy into my surroundings. Of course I had no idea that it was an AuraTransformation™ that was about to take place.

My friend was almost in a trance during the healing but fortunately, because of my psychic abilities, I was able to keep myself oriented during the procedure, in which my spiritual consciousness became fully connected to my body. This method, quickly seized upon by the majority of my clients over a short period of time, then became the basis for bringing the New Time energy to many people.

Where Are We Going?

The world and our lives are always going somewhere new. That is what spirit and life do as they are in constant motion.

It is only through the compressed materiality and matter on this Earth that things can remain stable and retain their shape and structure over a very long time.

If people are able to keep themselves as still as the very heaviest matter then life is not possible. If people are entirely or partially stuck, be it emotionally, mentally or bodily and do not understand or are unable to flow with the eternal life-stream, life is blocked and physical and mental imbalances occur.

It is therefore crucial to remain in constant inner motion as this gives optimal living conditions for the spirit. It is also essential to remember to rest the physical body on a regular basis, so that the battery does not run flat. The mind does not get tired, as it can easily stay awake if something interests it enough.

People's need for sleep and rest is entirely due to the body and brain, as these two work hard at feeding the system, creating the framework and holding together the whole system.

How many people in love sleep all the time? Not many, because they would rather be living and feeling and floating around in their mental state of pure pleasure. The body's basic need for rest has to be met at some other time when life, the spirit and energy are not quite so intensely occupied. It is very interesting to note that your body is not in fact really tired if life and love are pulsing through it at full speed. Life and the spirit are the very essence of existence and are indeed its elixir. They can keep the body and the whole system running at full steam and therefore create the basis for a longer physical life than if everything in the system were running in a slower, heavier or more depressed way.

No-one suddenly decides they need a good sleep after the first intense period of being in love has passed. Getting rest is not a problem if the mind is lively and happy.
Spirit is life and when life is flowing in a positive way, it creates the conditions that allow spirit to give your body stronger life energy and greater happiness than usual.

So, where are we humans headed now?

We are on the way to creating more space in our human systems so that spirit energy and life can enter into us to the fullest degree. When we look at the small children whose completely new energies are flowing to Earth at this time, we can see energies that cannot be suppressed by anything other than the body's physical limitations or adult human ignorance and lack of understanding of the inner structure that these new creatures are equipped with from birth.

Outwardly these children are pretty small in size and may not yet be able to speak or understand adult language completely but inside, they are often equipped with a far greater spiritual capacity than their parents or other adults.

As adults we must therefore learn to accommodate the fact that children in particular and we too of course, can make spirit blossom in an optimal way through the body so that we can live life to the full. We also need to help children accept that they have to function within the 'old' existing frameworks and structures within society until they have been changed so much that they are perfectly in tune with the New Time energy. Then, children will be able to internally identify with them.

The world is now constantly moving in the direction of ever-increasing New Time energy. Therefore, the parents of a New Time child have a major responsibility to bear, though fortunately there are a lot of them to share this responsibility if they are open to doing so.

As adults represent the bridge between the old and the new times, they need to teach their children to live with a physical and spiritual balance in their lives where the adults themselves are a product of the old time outer-focused energy, which is based on everything that can be seen, heard and felt.

Unlike adults, children of today arrive here with an internally-guided intuitive and totally unstructured spirit energy and life force embedded directly in their systems. This is fully visible to even the most limited of adults. Adults will need to learn to embrace this energy as their own and not relate to it as if it were undesirable and to be suppressed or eliminated as soon as possible.

The New Time children are, in general, very intelligent children with great human insight and through their openness to everything new, they are able to help inspire their parents and other adults in their personal growth. However adults need to be open and positive towards the children's input in their daily lives.

Anyone can see that the New Time children are different from the children of previous times because these children are so full of life that it is almost too much for their parents, teachers and adult acquaintances when they truly open up. If the adults do not have any New Time energy in them, their systems can 'short circuit' several times a day as they try to accommodate the children's internal and external rapidity. It is a fact that these children are here to stay and that there will continue to be more of them, since adults themselves choose to bring them into this world. It is therefore up to the adults to find quick and effective solutions to any cooperation and communication problems across the generations.

The New Time Energy

The New Time is here to stay, as is the energy with which all the new children are arriving. The adult population therefore needs to show much greater flexibility in allowing these new and unstructured energies into their lives more efficiently than they have done so far. At the same time adults need to be much more on their toes regarding the setting of their personal boundaries in relation to these new children.

A new era has begun where children's energies are in many cases much stronger than their parents', which is why the parents must have boundary setting and consistency as important tools in their personal toolbox.

New Time children must obviously not be allowed to overwhelm the adults with their strong, often uninhibited and boundary-crossing energies and language, although nowadays this is unfortunately the case in many places in the world.

Both children and adults need to show each other respect.

Looking at the positive aspects of the integration of these unstructured New Time energies, it is evident that many adults in the future will have to reassess their parenting and also their own attitude to the world. Children function as excellent eye-openers for adults, particularly their parents, since they often mirror the adult's behaviour, right down to the smallest detail. Unfortunately children just do not use the delete key on the keyboard, which is why the parents' less fortunate characteristics can quickly show up in the behaviour of their children!

If your children seem to reflect some of the personal traits that you cannot accept in yourself and do not feel good about, you could start by looking at yourself and changing things within, then you will be able to start positively imprinting on your child.

New Time children must often be helped to understand and respect the customary ways of doing things both in the community and at home in the family. When and only when this understanding is in place, can they begin to be consulted or have any input at home or in their immediate environment. They will then come up with lots of constructive proposals for changes, especially the kinds that involve making short cuts.

Children must be able to manage their own energy before they can hope to have greater influence over their own lives and surroundings. As the amount of energy that these new children bring is not tiny, to say the least, the energies must not be released prematurely into the community without supervision and without the necessary self–control in place. That would be like allowing a swarm of bees to come in through the front door of your home – and what's more, you will have invited the problems inside yourself.

Parents of New Time children should therefore ensure that the children can manage their own personal on/off switch safely before they are let loose into the big wide world. This is a responsibility that more and more parents are coming to realize the further we move into the New Time, where honesty, direct confrontation, consistency and accountability become the daily routine for many people.

When adults choose to have children in this time, they cannot afford just to allow a part of their child into their hearts just because they cannot accommodate the being of the entire child. It is the whole child or no child, otherwise they should choose instead to delegate full responsibility to others and then not expect to get a free pass as a parent later in life when others have done all of the parenting work for them.

New Time children are in fact just as loyal to their teachers in life as previous children were to even the most irresponsible parents.

Today, parents have no guarantee that their children will be attached to them for life unless they act in a positive way as the child grows up, which is, of course, quite fair. You do not get attention and energy from your children by simply being their biological parents but rather from the good that you bring to their lives.

In the future, the spirit and the body will be one. People who are close to each other in their hearts and who always act from the impulses of the heart will be the ones who follow each other both in spirit and in physical life.

Indigo Children

Indigo children is the term used to describe all the children born in the period from 1995 up to and including 2008. These children are born with an indigo-coloured aura – see the illustration on page 79 – and they are born as open energy channels that can channel cosmic energy for themselves and for others at any time through either healing or human contact. They are born healers and have a great desire to help both humans and animals, simply because they cannot help it but also because they are secretly longing to be recognized by adults because of their immense human potential. It is children and young people who are often unconsciously working very hard to create an open connection between the heavenly and the earthly in adult lives – and especially in their parents' lives.

They act as bridge builders between the old and the new times, as well as being ambassadors for the New Time energy.

Indigo children are self-taught and they are not slow at imitating exactly the people around them or finding new ways of doing things themselves. They can often seem antisocial and enormously provocative to the people around them due to their lack of boundaries and total lack of respect for many things.

Indigos have no obedience to authority and do not like established systems. They have no respect for adults who have no respect for themselves, which is something they can feel at a distance in exactly the same way that animals can.

Indigos are born with complete internal balance, although it does not always look this way to adult eyes. They are therefore so honest and truth-seeking deep within themselves that they cannot lie, either to themselves or to others. Their sometimes provocative actions in relation to the outside world are not car-

ried out with bad intentions. Rather, this is a sign of powerless-
ness in relation to the situation in question, where balance is
lacking and the adults do not appear to be reacting.

**Indigos have strong intuition and find it very difficult
to lie to themselves, because the body will quite simply
'reveal' everything or decide to go on strike. Whenever
they themselves or others try to force them into doing
something they do not really want to do or do not feel
happy doing, they can get stomach aches, headaches or
neck pain, especially if their limits are not respected in
one way or another.**

Indigo children are born with strong self-esteem and believe in
themselves and their own abilities. Therefore they are fully con-
vinced that everyone else, especially their parents, are fascinated
by hearing their personal version of a particular story, so there
is often a great deal of talking in the company of Indigo children.

Generally speaking, they are not afraid of much, because they
think they can do everything themselves at a very early age. In
fact they can sometimes be quite a danger to themselves because
they do not yet understand the body's physical limitations but
on the other hand, they are complete masters of their spiritual
potential right from birth. This can create some problems for
the child's inner self image in the early years.

Since Indigo children have no karma, they have zero data in their
consciousness in terms of life experience, so they very often
have to get hurt before they realize and learn that they probably
should listen to what adults have to say. Slowly, they build up
respect for their parents and other adults, although adults with
the old time aura generally have less spirit and consciousness
potential than Indigo children, which is something that the child-

ren are fully aware of internally.

Nowadays not all adults have just the old time energy surrounding them. There are plenty of adult Indigos around who have always had the Indigo energy lying dormant in their consciousness. The old time aura structure which surrounds them since birth does not match their true energy identity.

It is characteristic of the majority of Indigo children and Indigo adults that their overall mission in life is to draw attention to any imbalances in their environment and in society in general in one way or another. They are often very skillful at dropping the hint to those around them that something needs to be changed both at home and within the self.

The Indigo Aura and the Balance Body

The Indigo aura consists of the physical body, the balance body and the spirit body, which corresponds to the higher mental body in the old time aura

The balance body is indigo coloured and consists of three strong energy focuses, namely the Hara chakra, the Heart chakra and the Pineal chakra, also called the third eye, which is described in the chapter *The Three Aura Structures* later in the book.

It is the balance body's indigo-coloured structure that is the basis for the concept of the Indigo aura. The balance body appears as a giant, deep violet or indigo-coloured membrane or diving suit containing a mass of sparks in various colours. The balance body is connected to the body itself without any kind of opening anywhere and the presence of the mass of different coloured sparks in the aura is so that the aura can continuously change its colour and energy expression depending on the person's mood and needs.

The balance body in the Indigo aura is both ultra-magnetic and ultra-protective. It connects the spirit body, which is located farther out in the aura where the intuition is, directly to the physical body so that the spirit and body can communicate appropriately with each other.

The main purpose of the balance body is to create balance within the child and its simultaneous direct connection with the spirit and the body means that it is only a short step from thought to action in the life of an Indigo child.

The balance body in the Indigo aura is semi-permeable, allowing for the easy penetration of spirit energy into the body thus creating strong feelings in the child about certain situations. Simultaneously, the body can easily send messages out into the spiritual sphere about its needs, which then has the intuition to send signals back to the body about what has to be done specifically to meet those needs.

This leaves us with some very sensitive children and adolescents who are in touch with their bodies, their thoughts and their feelings. This is why parents should be very aware of what they offer these children in terms of their diet and psychological conditions in daily life.

Indigo children and young people have a greater need for healthy eating and healthy living habits than people with the old time energy, simply because they are so sensitive to all outside influences.

They often get allergies and eczema just from the slightest imbalance in the immediate environment and many Indigos cannot tolerate smoke. They simply cannot keep their minds clear in smoke because it pollutes their spirit energy. This may sound absurd to many people but it is nonetheless the truth for many Indigo people.

Indigos also react positively to almost all natural medicines and alternative treatments.

The balance body allows Indigos to attract certain people and circumstances into their lives through the strength of their thought and willpower. Similarly, the balance body makes it possible for them to keep certain people and circumstances at a distance if they should wish to do so.

Indigos are good at setting boundaries in their lives but the children in particular do not always know exactly how to set appropriate boundaries, so training and life experience are needed before they can make proper use of their boundary-setting abilities.

Indigo children and young people are generally very open in relation to other people and it is easy for the people around them to read their thoughts and desires simply by looking at them. The energy around them in a given moment says simply everything about their state of mind, which is why the people around them often do not even have to bother asking them how they are feeling.

It is also easy to read whether they have a positive or negative view on certain people in their lives and they often express their opinions directly and without mercy, as honesty is a high priority in their lives.

Crystal Children

2009 – Pure Crystal Individual Children are Born

All children who came into the world from 2009 to 2012-13 were born with a fully developed Crystal aura and Crystal body.

In the period from 2004-2008, all children were born with a mixture of the Indigo and Crystal auras and the closer to 2009 the children are born, the cleaner the Crystal aura they are born with and the more crystallized they are in the body, which is why they are called Crystal individuals.

Depending on each child's upbringing and the amount of focus on consciousness development at home and/or in the child's immediate environment, the combined Indigo-Crystal aura will evolve all by itself at its own pace and at latest, by adulthood, it will have become a pure Crystal aura.

2012-13 – Pure Crystal Children are Born

All children born from 2012-2013 onwards are called 'true' Crystal people, because they are also crystallized in their network energy, which has an impact on their socialization capacities.

Cosmic Sources and Energy Copying

Crystal children are completely *pure cosmic sources* and are therefore a *totally closed circuit* within themselves. Other people can mirror themselves in them but they cannot take energy from them.

Crystal children do *not* function as channels for the highest cosmic forces in the same way that Indigo children do. Indigo children channel all cosmic energy down through their own aura and body and then transfer the energy to other people through healing, body contact, conversation, etc.

A *cosmic source* is a closed circuit with its origin in the heart and you can only become a source if you have your Heart chakra as your single activated chakra and the only strong energy focus in the body left over from the original seven chakras belonging to the old time soul aura.

By contrast, Indigo children have three chakras in their aura – the Pineal chakra, Heart chakra and Hara chakra – representing a stage of awareness midway between the old time soul energy and the new Crystal energy.

Under normal conditions, Crystal individuals and Crystal humans are self-recharging closed circuits capable of charging themselves completely as long as there is peace and balance around them in daily life.

Crystal children often need only a very short period of time to raise their energy frequency if they have been in low frequency and energy-intensive environments or if they have been with people who have attempted to steal some of their energy, even though no-one actually can.

It is just *not* possible to steal energy from Crystal children. However if the people around them have run completely flat, they can 'copy' the children's energy expression so much - as if they were using a photocopier to copy everything in a single batch - that the Crystal child's 'machinery' can become over-heated and risk breaking down.

If the energy of a Crystal child is completely flat because the cosmic source has been worn down due to other people's copy-ing, the child must be left in peace for a period of time just like a photocopier, so it can be recharged again.

If a quick charge of energy is needed, it can be done through contact or conversation with another cosmic source – in other words by copying from another Crystal person – and then the system will be able to quickly recharge itself so that the child will soon be ready to go out into the world again, fully charged.

One of the common life purposes of Crystal children is to let their parents and other adults 'copy' their energies and perso-nal attitudes and needs. Therefore it is expected that parents in particular, as well as educators, carers and politicians etc., will be able to transform society to meet future needs, within a reasonable timescale, for when the New Time high frequency energies make even more serious headway on Earth.

Unfortunately, one of the problems with energy copying is that it is rarely the case that a single copy or a few copies are made of the Crystal child's consciousness qualities during a full day. It would be fine if this were the case.

Many adults do not have the consciousness capacities needed to implement the new Crystal energies in their minds, which is why Crystal children end up being copied again and again by their parents and educators and others, who feed on their energy and therefore they can become run down in their energy system after 'just' normal contact with adults.

In the periods when Crystal children end up totally run-down with no energy and a system 'burn out', it will take a huge push of consciousness from the outside to quickly get their energy up and running again. Healing, reflexology and cranial sacral therapy, etc., can be used to get the child back into shape but often parents continue to 'energy-copy' the child anyway, as they are deliberately working to expand their own consciousness.

However, these days, it is not only parents with whom children have daily contact. It is therefore of utmost importance to find out who your children have contact with in their daily life. Are they people with a relatively low energy level that are likely to copy the child constantly without even knowing it, or are they well-stimulated people who have something to contribute to the child's experience? Even though today's children have a clear mission in life here on Earth with regard to their parents and the older generation, they should not be run flat in their day-to-day lives.

Just as adults should not go to work just to return home completely burnt out.

Although Crystal children are pure cosmic sources, they are still children with all the relationships and opportunities that exist for their age group. These children still have to learn all the usual earthly rules of the game through their parents and adult care-givers. Crystal children are far more certain about what they want and do not want than children have been in the past, because truth is fully integrated into their hearts.

The Transition from the Indigo to the Crystal Aura

The difference between the Crystal aura and the Indigo aura is that the spirit energy of Crystal children is located inside the body as an enhanced life force, whereas the spirit energy of Indigo children is located outside the body as an enhanced radiance.

When the Indigo aura is ready to be transformed into a Crystal aura, the balance body and the spirit body in the Indigo aura begin to merge into a single energy body, whose colour and texture change from being a strong magnetic indigo-coloured force into a more delicate pinkish-purple crystalline diamond colour with crystal-clear and visibly shimmering radiance. Although the Crystal aura appears to be weak and fragile compared to the Indigo aura, it is, in fact, much stronger in its energy structure than the Indigo aura.

Following the crystallization process in the aura, the body begins to crystallize in a similar way and a large part of the spirit energy, which was previously located in the spirit body on the outer edge of the Indigo aura, moves through the newly created Crystal aura and into the body in order to upgrade the energy there. You can read about this in my two books *"The Crystal Human and the Crystallization Process Part I"* and *"Part II"*, which discuss this process in more detail.

You can see the Crystal aura illustrated in the chapter *The Three Aura Structures* on page 81.

The Characteristics of Crystal Children

It is characteristic of all Crystal children that they are very clear in their energies, honest by nature and extremely truth-seeking in their dealings with other people. They do not package things neatly just for the sake of the people around them.

Unlike Indigo children, Crystal children are completely lacking in the boundary-setting blue energy in their aura structure. This is not a problem for the children themselves, as they are very conscious about what they like and do not like and who it is good for them to be with. They are therefore not willing to compromise in any context at all. They would prefer to isolate themselves from the outside world if they consider themselves to be the only acceptable company for miles around.

Neither the parents nor the immediate family should feel too complacent in the Crystal child's presence. These new children do not associate voluntarily with people with a limited mind-set or with people who have controlling and/or disruptive energies. If the power is too strong however and the parents decide on something other than what the child wants, you can be quite sure that soon 'feverish' conditions and chaos will arise in the environment. Deep within them, Crystal children carry a strong internal fire that can make anything negative around them burn up completely.

At an unconscious level, Crystal children can quickly drive the people around them up the wall in one way or another, without it being clearly visible who is actually pulling the strings. These children do not want to be limited by their parents just because they cannot keep up with their children's rapid development of consciousness on both the inner and outer level. It is a fact that the new children often do not understand the slow and sometimes complicated way of life followed by many adults with the old-time energy structure and so there is a strong need for boundary setting and a willingness for the parents to explain things clearly in order to get the children to accept and understand the adults' way of doing things.

Children of the future only use the shortcut keys on the keyboard and they have no wish to use any old-fashioned methods from the time when their parents were children.

Boundary setting, consistency, accountability, direct confrontation and telling the truth are therefore the key expressions in New Time child-raising, which is why, in the future, the focus will be on providing clear and concise explanations to children about *why* and *why not* rather than on the parents' total absorption in the child's universe and the desire to comply with all of the child's wishes in life.

Respect for the individual child and simple explanations for everything will get you very far in communication with New Time children, as they are very concrete in their quest for answers to both big and small questions. If they seek affection and caring, they are correspondingly specific in their quest to get their needs met. Everything proceeds in a very easy and straightforward way, as long as the people around them can keep up with the Crystal children's pace and insight.

Fire Children with Pure Willpower

Of the four elements Earth, Air, Water and Fire, Crystal children represent the Fire energy and thus pure willpower. They are truly passionate about whatever feels right for them. In fact it is totally impossible for them not to be like that.

But it is not only the children's spirit energy that is on fire. Since the spirit is inside the body, it means that Crystal children have a correspondingly high internal heat. So they will often prefer warm water in the bathtub instead of hot water and throw off the duvet even on a cold winter night.

There are not a lot of different emotions in the Crystal child's life, as emotions are actually just different ways of expressing one's personal viewpoint. Crystal children are much more simple and straightforward in expressing themselves than their parents and they convey quite clearly whether they are satisfied with a situation or not. They do not like to submit their bodies to a lot of hormonal stress brought on by widely differing emotions. They are happy, angry or sad. Things do not need to be any more complicated than that.

On the other hand, they want to have all the different possibilities of human relationships explained to them, in order to better understand and relate to the adults in their life. In particular, they like to have explanations as to why many adults have so many different kinds of reactions to everything.

The new children are far clearer and more direct by nature than the majority of adults, who often let their thoughts, feelings and actions run away with them. If there is something that these children do not want to do, it can take an enormous amount of sensible arguments to convince them that they actually have to do as they are told.

Many adults will probably perceive Crystal children as being extremely stubborn, which - indeed they are – but they are not stubborn just for the sake of it. Because the spiritual fire is constantly burning in their hearts, it is impossible for them to lie to themselves or to others, so if the people around them are trying to divert them from their inner truth, their spirit energy is quickly transformed into a huge fire, which can destroy everyone and everything.

It might suddenly look as though these children have come

straight from the fires of Hell – although they actually represent the heavenly truth through their heart's flame. Pure spirit energy in full eruption is undeniably powerful stuff for most people.

It can be likened to a volcanic eruption on a small island, where it is totally impossible for those around to escape unharmed.

It can therefore be quite painful for the poor parents of New Time Crystal children when there is a crisis at home but they are also the world's luckiest parents when everything is running smoothly and the level of consciousness at home is high.

When there is total balance in a 'Crystal home' there is an unending stream of love from the children at all times, even when they are sleeping and it is almost like being in heaven having the children around. There is an overall cohesion and meaning to everything among the family members and the feeling of being a family unit with space for all of its members to be fully autonomous individuals is quite unique.

Crystal Children and their Parents

Crystal children have a very clear picture of who their mother and father are as people and the role that parents are expected to play in the child's life. As parents, you need to ensure that the relationship between mum and dad is both strong and loving enough to resist the child's very direct comments about relationships in the home and about the parents' relationship, because nothing ever gets swept under the carpet when a Crystal child is around!

> Crystal children notice absolutely any anomaly in their parents' relationship and in the home in general, no matter how small. Crystal children will articulate absolutely every observation that they make. Above all, the truth must be told, even if that might mean the parents' relationship as a couple is in the spotlight.

Crystal children will have no qualms about remarking that mum and dad do not fit together as a couple, if this happens to be the case. If mum and dad are not good together as a couple, they need to separate. If the parents get divorced, it does not automatically mean that the child must give up contact with both parents. In the inner universe of the Crystal child it is quite easy to keep their parents' two different worlds separate from each other if need be.

If their parents do get divorced, Crystal children have no problems accepting new 'parents' into their lives. The only requirement from the children is simply that the adult newcomers must possess positive human qualities and maybe even qualities that the children may benefit from integrating into their own personalities. New siblings and family members as a whole are not a problem, for the quality demands are the same, regardless of who the people are and what roles they are expected to play in the child's life.

Crystal children will always support their parents' life choices regarding a new partner and new family and friendship relations in the best possible way, as long as they sense that the parents feel better about themselves and that there is nothing covert or incorrect in these relationships.

Crystal children are very accommodating to all positive changes in their lives. However, they can pose a huge threat to parents if they feel that the people who the parents surround themselves with are not 'right' for either the parents or for themselves. If so, the child will completely shut down any cooperation and this is not a pleasant experience for any of the parties involved.

The Way to Say Goodbye

Crystal children are much more focused in their own energy than most other people. Because their spirit energy is present in the body, they always have their energy with them and once they have said goodbye to another person, they immediately turn their backs on them and concentrate instead on the new framework and opportunities that are ahead of them.

Crystal children will never mistakenly leave a portion of their energy with other people, not even with their parents, when the child and the parents are separated from each other during the course of the day.

Crystal children do not long for someone or something that is not within their reach, even though it may be a long time before they see their parents or best friends again.

The children themselves have a good sense of whether it is worthwhile wishing to be in another place or not, for if the possibility of getting to that place or those persons is totally out of the question, it is as though there is nothing more to do in that situation. Then it is just a pure waste of the child's energy to think any more along those tracks and the child is very aware of this him or herself at an early age.

The New Children and Health

Many pregnant women get physically unwell and suffer from very bad vomiting when they are expecting a New Time child.

The number of pregnant women that take sick leave and their degree of nausea during pregnancy, is now far greater than before.

On an energy level, everything is rearranged inside them because the child's energies are so strong and have so much information contained in them that the mother cannot keep up with such an energy system, especially in her own body.

The New Time mother must be very high frequency in order to have any hope of having a relatively trouble-free pregnancy.

When young children get eczema, allergies and severe fever, it usually indicates that the parents' energy is too far below that of the child. The child is not being met in the very high frequency energies with which it has come into the world and the illness can then be used to get parents to wake up and be made aware of the importance of the New Time energy as opposed to the old time energy that the parents have grew up with.

For many parents of young children, a whole new world will open up, thanks to the child's illness because it forces them to reassess life in many different and often very relevant ways.

Many Crystal children have problems with their ears, because they have to move down in the energy spectrum to meet their parents at their energy level. This is similar to being lowered down to the ocean floor without taking into account the different pressure underwater. As soon as the contact is over, the Crystal diver automatically rises to the surface to take in his/her own element and breathe energy in a frequency that is more natural.

Only above the water is there a natural balance in the head but unfortunately most communication with the outside world takes place deep in the water. So unless the person wants to isolate themselves from others, repeated ascents and descents are necessary and this will inevitably result in problems with the ears and a feeling of lack of balance in the head.

> At times, New Time children can have higher body temperatures than other people without actually being ill.

The heat and the periodically greatly increased body temperature help to quickly raise the children's energy levels, each time the people around them have been copying their energy too much.

It should be clear that many adults, especially elderly people, can charge up their personal batteries to an incredible degree through contact with New Time children, who are completely clean in their energies and thus represent the very latest model of consciousness on the market. The elderly often hope, without even being conscious of it, that without using too many of their own resources, they can get additional energy through children and that they can stay young in mind through on-going contact with the new children.

It is now up to the older generation to do something in their own lives to improve the quality of life and ensure a permanent influx of New Time energy into their energy structure and aura. This is discussed later in the book in the chapters *You Must Help the Development Yourself* and *New Healing Methods for Personal Growth* and in the main chapter *AuraTransformation™*.

Crystal Children versus Indigo Children

The aura of a Crystal child does not appear to be as big as that of an Indigo child. However, Crystal children have a great inner strength and an understanding of the connections between all things. Their personal strength and spiritual foothold is much stronger than those of Indigo children.

Indigo children are exclusively associated with their spirit consciousness via the balance body, through which they experience an ongoing collaboration between the spirit and the body but they are not at one with their spirit in the same way that Crystal children are.

In fact the qualities of the Indigo balance body are still present in the Crystal aura but because the spirit energy is fused with the Indigo balance body, the Crystal aura appears and functions in a different way from the Indigo aura.

> **Indigo children use their intuition and spirit energy in the aura to sense whether things are right or wrong. Crystal children *know* if things are right or wrong because they use their spiritual awareness in both the aura and the body to register it, which means that there is a kind of simultaneous 'double registering'.**

To recapitulate: when we compare the auras of Indigo children and Crystal children, the far higher frequency energies of the Crystal child's aura make the aura appear lighter than the Indigo child's balance body. The Crystal aura is transparent and appears in a shimmering crystal violet colour with a pink undertone and does not have the direct blue protective energy within it, as the Indigo balance body does.

Crystal children do not need to protect their personal energy from the outside world, because their spirit energy is fully integrated into the body and therefore cannot mistakenly act as an enhanced vitality for others. Not even if other people physically interfere with them.

We all know that physical assaults on children continue to take place. Fortunately this is legislated against in most places in the world so that society can come up with practical solutions against those carrying out the assault. Indigo children and especially Crystal children tend not find themselves victims of psychological abuse without rejecting it either directly or via adults other than their own parents.

In the world of Crystal children, there is no distinction between physical and psychological abuse, as both kinds of abuse are experienced in the same way in both aura and body. In the future, the truth about everything's real connection with everything else will be revealed more rapidly than has ever previously been the case. Adults will, in general, find it very difficult to approach the strong energies of small Crystal children if they do not have honourable intentions towards them. The high-frequency balance energy of the new children will illuminate everything in their surroundings and adults with malicious intentions will appear as being very wrong in their energy, which is indeed the case.

'True' Crystal children will be born in their ultimate pure form from 2012 onwards, when all children will be born with a high frequency and bright Crystal aura and body and with a fully developed crystal network integrated into their consciousness from birth.

This means, among other things, that the children's energies are freed from the energies of their parents and especially from their mother's energies, at a much earlier age than in the past.

There is now no longer a so-called symbiosis or total cohesion between parents and children right up to puberty. This was a connection that previously led many young people to break away from their parents' energies in an often inappropriate and violent way, so that they could become independent individuals, creating their own identity outside the family framework and away from parental energies.

The energies of Crystal children will free themselves from the parents' auras around the age of 3-4, which of course is very early compared to past parent-child relationships. From a pure consciousness perspective, Crystal children are ready to stand on their own two feet at this early stage, which will result in major problems between parents and children if the parents try to resist the self-liberation of their child's consciousness.

Who said that it would be easy to be parents in the future? There will certainly be no possibility for parents to hide behind the many daily activities of their family and especially their children rather than living their own adult lives, as Crystal children are basically only receptive to learning and getting advice from strong adults who have respect for themselves and who live their lives to the full. As an alternative, the children would rather prefer to be alone or be in the company of completely different people.

This is probably why the majority of women in the future may choose to have children at a relatively late age, maybe in their forties, which is not so late when you consider that people in the future will live longer with each decade that passes. It is highly desirable that both men and women create their own personal life foundations and live their lives fully before they decide to bring children into the world.

As I said before, in the future, no parents will live their lives through their children and if they have proven themselves as adults before they have children, they can better guide their children regarding the consequences of various life choices.

The energies of Indigo children will free themselves from the parental aura at around the age of 7-8, which is when they have started at school. At this age, they have after-school clubs and activities and have usually created their own little circle of acquaintances independently of their parents.

It is characteristic of most Indigo children who have had their personal energies freed from parental energies that they have a great desire to help other people. This is because they want to but also because they just cannot help it. As mentioned previously, they also seek recognition from those around them and especially from adults. It feels a lot fairer to Indigo children that they are proclaimed as today's wonder children when they feel that they have earned it through good deeds.

Inside every Indigo child there lives a saving heavenly angel but there is also a wicked demon who will draw attention to himself in the most inappropriate ways, if the child is in a bad mood.

Crystal children do not have the same built-in craving and desire to help other people that Indigo children have. However, they always know whether the people around them really need help or not, although they will only help if it feels right for them to do so.

Crystal children do not have the Indigo children's underlying need to save the world. If other people need their help, these people must take the initiative to ask them, as Crystal children will not, as a matter of course, help others without being asked first.

Transition Children

The term *transition children* is used for the young people and adults born between 1987 and 1994 when parts of the Indigo energy became more and more integrated into the auras of all newborn children even though they were born with the old time aura structure. However different conditions apply to children born in the periods 1992-1994 and 1987-1991:

1992-94

In the period from 1992 until the end of 1994, all children were born with a so-called mixed aura containing very large parts of the Indigo energy and a smaller portion of soul energy.

These children, who are now young adults, have a lot of the New Time materialization power in them but they are not fully protected and lack the ability to set reasonable boundaries for themselves and others. They therefore have difficulty finding balance within themselves.

Young people born in this period can be very assertive and direct in relation to those around them but they are not strong enough to take back in return that they send out to others. This type of behaviour may cause great mental distress to both them and the people around them and often means that their parents must tiptoe around when dealing with them, in order not to step too far over their invisible boundaries.

Conversely, parents can have the feeling of being completely fooled by these very same 'vulnerable' young people, who are not slow to exploit their parents' kind-heartedness in any situation, if the young person is having a good day and feels that they have the psychological upper hand. This is a tendency that is very likely to continue into the transition child's adult life if the parents do not try to stop it from happening.

Unfortunately, due to their great emotional fluctuations, there will have been many occasions during their upbringing when these young people will have helped to make their parents look completely wrong in the eyes of others, no matter what positive steps the parents have made to understand the sometimes troubled mind of their offspring.

When children and young people lack inner balance it spreads instantly to all those around them in their daily life and this in turn creates external imbalance that will have to be dealt with by a parent or by both parents.

1987-91

Children born from summer 1987 to the end of 1991, as well as some of those born in the mid-1980s, were all born with a mixed aura containing a small portion of Indigo energy and a greater proportion of soul energy.

It is, therefore, very difficult for them to choose whether they should stick to the accepted path and be neat and well-mannered, or whether they should be rebellious and go entirely their own way in life. Their protection against the outside world is not that strong, so they often end up by adopting their parent's or other adult role model's ideals and ways of doing things although deep down they have strong thoughts of wanting to do something else.

These young people may seem very calm and happy – especially in their parents' eyes – but they often lack decisiveness. Experience has shown that if they get their auras upgraded to a Crystal aura, which you can read about in the chapters *New Healing Methods for Personal Growth* and *AuraTransformation™*, then things can really take off for them. In a short period of time, a completely new, stronger personality will step forward, to the amazement of those around them.

A golden rule for parents bringing up and supervising young people with the transition energy is that even though these youngsters appear to be adults before their time, they are rarely ready to take full responsibility for themselves and their own lives. Parents should therefore not neglect their responsibility and supervision of these young people too early. Not even after they have left home.

This parental rule applies in general to all New Time children – it is not a good idea to let children decide when to go to bed at night because the influx of high-frequency energy in their aura often makes them unable to determine when the day is over and it is time for them to say goodnight.

New Time children and young people can continue being active long after midnight without any problem but this also means that they can sleep all the next morning, which they often do – sprawled across the desk at school, to the great displeasure of their teachers.

Often these young people are also completely uncritical of what information they receive from their computer or TV, as well as how much time they spend on them, so continuous parental advice and supervision is recommended.

Consciousness Expansion

The Influx of New Energies

The influx of new energies to Earth is helping to get people to rely more on their own intuition and feelings regarding the connections between things, both visible and invisible, because everyone really knows the answers to everything deep within themselves. It is then 'simply' a question of reaching inside to find your own answers. This can, of course be problematic if there has been negative personal imprinting and history which block the path since everyone is influenced by their own life history and upbringing and so they will usually see the world through glasses that are coloured by this.

So if you want answers to questions about a particular situation, you can either seek the answer inside yourself or seek out other people who match your own energies and get them to answer the questions. The more you can reconcile yourself with another person's personal expression, the less resistance there will be from inside yourself to the answers they may come up with.

We always know what is best for ourselves, although we can often be our own worst enemy when the right answer appears and the time comes to act on it in real life. Often we do not like to hear the truth, or it feels like the wrong time to deal with the truth in real life.

Apart from the question of timing, the new high-frequency energies can help to open up the individual's desire and willingness to take personal responsibility for their own life. If you dare to take responsibility for your own life, you are usually also willing to seek the right answers to your questions the first time a problem occurs.

Why drag things out for a long time, if you can get an honest answer right away that can be translated into concrete action?

Taking responsibility for your own life and being ready to use your intuition to get to the truth right away, these are the key concepts behind the influx of the very high frequency energies that is taking place on Earth at this time. Just look at today's children and how they translate these overall spiritual impulses into action, often to the great wonder and astonishment of their parents. Where on earth can the children be getting it from? How can today's children and young people deal with and accept so much in life relating to such things as divorce, death and personal crises without going to pieces inside? Many adults would simply be shattered by such situations. Children are really not old enough to understand or relate to the fact that the world around them is falling apart – or are they?

The conclusion regarding the influx of the New Time energy is that in stressful situations, today's children and young people often behave in a far more adult and realistic way than their parents. How can that be? It is because these children intuitively know whether or not things are hanging together properly in any situation, and they follow their inner truth rather than the one that the adults have taught them to follow, unless, of course, the two truths coincide.

Children of today feel no inner joy at seeing their parents together if the parents are not really fond of each other and radiate love in each other's presence. If the situation is not optimal, which children are often much more aware of than you might think, then a divorce is clearly preferable from the children's point of view, although it may be hard having to move house and change friends.

Although children might be very sad when divorce becomes a reality, they will express themselves with just as much joy and confidence as soon as their parents have peace in the new framework they have chosen for their lives.

New Time children will not be fooled in the same way as their parents into believing that a situation is better than it actually is. So it is better to change things, even if changing is difficult and might bring uncertainty. At the same time this could create a basis for exploring the whole world in a completely new way and as adults we should not underestimate the value of this in relation to our children.

New Time children are creative and are always thinking of new possibilities and new ways of doing things, so they will be able to make their way through various joys, sorrows and life crises. In the future, many things will run at a faster pace than before, as all the Indigo and Crystal children, as a part of their common overall life task, will press their parents to use all the shortcut keys on their personal keyboards. This will inevitably speed up the tempo in society.

In the future, no-one anywhere will be rewarded for wearing themselves out, either physically or mentally, unless it is for something they want and are comfortable with. Struggling too hard to achieve one's goal or taking a longer route than necessary to achieve the goal will be something that belongs exclusively to the past and it will be something that today's children and tomorrow's adults will not even be able to relate to or understand.

You Must Help the Development Yourself

In the spiritual world there has been awareness for many years that around the year 2000 the Earth would go into the New Time but only very few people understood that the new influx of consciousness to the Earth would require a concrete effort from every single adult person.

Many people believed that in the New Time they should solely focus on *thinking positively* and *living healthily* but unfortunately this is not enough for everyone. Of course, positive thinking and healthy living are good things but now an overall shift in consciousness in the minds of most adults is also necessary. The New Time energy is not only about children.

From the point of view of consciousness, the New Time energy represents a completely different, more energetic and love-oriented energy influx into our planet than we have been accustomed to. This influx affects everyone on Earth and was going on long before the actual millennium change, right back to the mid-1980s.

The New Time energy came to Earth all by itself but it does not slip into people's energy systems all by itself.

The energy will lead to everyone integrating new values into their lives, each at their own speed, thereby acquiring new ways of living. In order for the New Time values to get a reasonable force of penetration among the Earth's population as a whole, it will be necessary, in the meantime, for the frequency level of the Earth and its population to increase sharply in order to match the new energy influx. However, this will not happen by itself, contrary to what many people may hope and believe. There must be a manifesting force from the outside in the form of a therapist to attach the energy in the new aura to the body.

The old time karma-driven soul energy must be replaced with

the New Time free and unstructured spirit energy, so that adults can acquire the value norms of either the Indigo or Crystal energy and have it fully integrated into their consciousness and thereby achieve a balance between their inner and outer personality.

The only people who do not need to change the value norms of their consciousness system are the Indigo and Crystal children and young Indigo children, as they are born with the New Time aura structure fully integrated from birth.

The New Time Indigo and Crystal energies do not just appear by themselves. They must be chosen consciously. Therefore no adults with the old time aura structure will have the experience of waking up one morning and being completely transformed, so that they are pure Indigo or Crystal people. It is simply not possible to materialize the New Time aura structure oneself so that it surrounds the body permanently.

People with a soul aura may well attract the Indigo and Crystal energy themselves but they *cannot* maintain the energy permanently in their aura without constantly having to stay focused on this, which would naturally take their focus from other important things in their life.

There *must* be a materializing force from the outside, which itself has the energy in place in order to connect the spirit energy with the body through the Indigo balance body or the Crystal aura.

If you want to go directly from the soul aura structure to the Crystal aura without your body being protected by your aura in the transitional period - the soul aura cannot transform by itself into an Indigo aura without the aura disappearing completely - then you run the risk of 'dying' in the metaphorical sense and physical illness and extreme psychological vulnerability is perhaps almost inevitable. If people with the soul aura invite the spirit energy directly into their body, with little warning, they could die. Not only in consciousness but also in the body, which means that they could become very weak and feel on the verge of death.

The New Time spirit energy is therefore not something to play around with or try to integrate purely out of curiosity.

If you wish to expand your consciousness, help is available from the new consciousness-expanding techniques and healing methods available on the market.

Today's adults need to send thoughts out into the world expressing the desire to get help with integrating the new energies into their consciousness. It often happens that soon after they will 'suddenly' see information about the new healing methods because they are themselves attracting this information. After that, it is up to them to act on the matter.

It is up to each individual adult person to decide and take responsibility as to whether they feel ready to change their aura structure and consciousness or not. No other person can or should assume this responsibility.

New Healing Methods for Personal Growth

As previously mentioned, the New Time energy is not only for children. It is for the present and the future of everyone. For many adults, however, it is quite difficult to accept that their personal energies are no longer aligned with the times. Often, the adults are active, fulfilled and good at their jobs and it is pretty frustrating to see themselves overtaken by children, both large and small, who can master a computer as if they were born with a manual inside them.

There is nothing concrete that you as an adult can do about

this situation, apart from perhaps taking a few extra computer courses! Of course, the new children constantly coming into the world are equipped with all the latest consciousness knowledge right from birth. This is knowledge that is only now being slowly made available to adults, as it begins to appear in the Earth's common or collective consciousness, of which we all are a part while we live on the planet. It is always possible for today's adults to change their own consciousness, if they really want to, so that they are more in harmony with children's energies.

Today there are various new healing and transformation methods that can contribute to the expansion of the adult's bodily and spiritual consciousness and allow them to receive the New Time Crystal energy fully integrated into their aura structure. It is primarily the Crystal energy that today's adults are upgrading to via their spiritual consciousness.

I have personally heard of the following techniques around the world: Kryon magnetization, DNA activation and AuraTransformation™, which I have developed myself and have helped to spread within Scandinavia and beyond. I have also heard of concepts such as Electromagnetic Field Balancing (also called the EMF Balancing technique), the Accelerating DNA Recoding Process and the Multidimensional Keys of Compassion.

In this book I will limit myself to discussing the effect of an AuraTransformation™, as I myself launched this transformation technique and therefore have an in-depth knowledge of the results from having such a treatment.

When is it Time for Consciousness Transformation?

So far I have only talked about an adult's consciousness-related need to change their aura structure, so that they can deal with their children and the world around them even better than before.

It can also be the case, however, especially as an adult, that if you are not good at registering your own internal and/or consciousness-related needs, then your body is happy to help you to recognize the fact that something is wrong somewhere in the system. It is therefore easy enough to ascertain what is physically wrong. The question then would be to know what is needed to change the various imbalances that often cannot be explained by doctors.

Here are a number of physical symptoms, often related to the hidden needs of the consciousness and aura to be expanded:

- Light sensitivity and stinging or red eyes
- Shortness of breath and an asthma-like condition
- Flu symptoms plus joint, bone and body pain associated with fever, where antibiotics do not work
- Itchy rash, eczema, sudden onset of allergies and hay fever
- Runny nose and sneezing when making the transition from warm to cold and vice versa
- Sore throat without being attacked by viruses and bacteria
- Ringing in the ears and tinnitus
- Dizziness, tiredness and fatigue, which come out of the blue
- Difficulty in sleeping and/or greater need for sleep than normal, irregular sleep patterns
- Migraine-like headache that does not respond to painkillers

Healing

Healing is not as abstract as many people think. In fact healing is the equivalent to using energy work in the form of thoughts, images and desires, etc. to try to influence a person, a feeling or other things to move in a certain direction.

Through energy work and healing, a healer tries to influence the client's energy system to get better, either by rearranging existing energies, removing energy or adding energy from outside.

The addition of healing, energy and balance to a person's energy system can happen in many different ways, which may be mental, emotional or physical.

It is, for example, possible to feel deep joy just by looking at the colour of the walls in a particular room or from the scent of wild flowers in a field. Similarly, it is always nice to have your back stroked by your beloved. The methods may differ greatly but the effects can be the same.

It is possible for almost everyone to heal and calm their own bodies, their thoughts and their own minds if they just find what is relaxing for them. It is just like when you have to find a way to get a little baby to stop crying. Either the child is hungry or tired, or it just needs attention, care, touching or presence. These needs can be naturally met by the caretakers. However, not many adults remember to really take care of themselves.

Most people associate healing with finding an alternative therapist so that the body and mind can be provided with extra energy and resources from outside, which is one of the things that happens with an AuraTransformation™.

AuraTransformation™ is More than Just Healing

The term alternative treatment covers a very broad spectrum of different therapies, all of which have in common that either the body or mind is encouraged in a natural way to regain its own balance. Alternative treatment is also based on influencing the life energy that everyone has within so that the body and mind can heal themselves from the inside out.

In the West, the alternative treatment world has almost always been in complete contradiction to everything that the established medical world has stood for. Today the strong divide between these initially conflicting sides has become less rigid regarding the different kinds of help available and the conditions for receiving this help.

AuraTransformation™ belongs in the category of alternative therapies, although it does not yet have the status of being registered as a form of alternative treatment. The Aura Mediator™, which is what the therapist is called, works through healing to consciously balance and strengthen the clients' physical, emotional and mental capacities, so that the clients feel better about themselves, their life and their body. However, AuraTransformation™ cannot be compared with any of the other healing forms that exist in the alternative therapy world, where the practitioner is usually trying to repair the existing aura if it is destroyed or damaged. Instead, AuraTransformation™ is a permanent change in one's aura and radiance and it works by upgrading the aura in order to achieve optimal balance between body and consciousness.

After the AuraTransformation™ your needs for help and energy from the world of alternative treatment will be largely limited to those therapies which involve the physical body in a very concrete way, such as massage, acupuncture, reflexology, Body-sds, cranio-sacral therapy and so on. After the AuraTransformation™, lying down and relaxing completely for half an hour will mean, in effect, that you charge yourself up internally and externally to a much greater extent than was possible with the old aura.

AuraTransformation™

What is an AuraTransformation™?

An AuraTransformation™ is a permanent change in one's aura and personal radiance. Instead of having the old type of aura that everyone used to be born with, the AuraTransformation™ will equip you with a new one - one that is fully updated and in tune with the New Time energy here on Earth, which was fully activated around the turn of the twentieth century.

The AuraTransformation™ can, over time, lead to many benefits on a personal level.

In short, the AuraTransformation™ connects your intuition to your decision-making capacity and enhances your personal charisma and radiance as well as your powers of manifestation. This is done by eliminating (dissolving) the old energy bodies – the etheric body, the astral body and the lower mental body – in the old aura, which is also called the soul aura. The energy in these energy bodies is transformed into an enhanced balance body as described in the chapter *Indigo Children*, or into an even stronger aura, as described in the chapter *Crystal Children* earlier in this book.

An AuraTransformation™ is performed by an Aura Mediator™, a therapist who maintains strong inner balance and who has a powerful ability to both dematerialize (dissolve) and materialize (augment) the energy in the aura.

An Aura Mediator™ works with 'balance energy' and in carrying out the AuraTransformation™ the Aura Mediator™ can so completely integrate balance into the client's system that the client will no longer be able to see the world and things around him or her as being black or white, or light and dark. Clients receive and achieve balance, both in their energy field, corresponding to their aura and radiance and they also acquire a deep inner balance that cannot be expressed in words.

This state of balance simply has to be experienced!

When choosing an Aura Mediator™, it is important to feel for yourself regarding who seems right for you. It is therefore important as a client to use your inner guidance when choosing one. As a rule, there will always be some small indication as to whether it should be one Aura Mediator™ or another, so you will not be in any doubt.

AuraTransformation™ is a method of consciousness transformation which seriously activates the influx of the New Time energy, so that it is only a short step from thought to action. However, it is absolutely not something that you should get done just to try it out. An AuraTransformation™ is a permanent and radical expansion of your consciousness and radiance and you cannot turn the clock back once it has been done.

If you become aura-transformed, feel it's a mistake and do not feel ready to live with the new high-frequency energies, this will often cause problems in your everyday life. You must be ready to accept your powers and have the will to take charge of what needs to be taken charge of in your life.

After an AuraTransformation™ you will begin in earnest to use all the shortcut keys on the keyboard but it is you who creates your own life story. There is no ghost writer hired to write your biography whilst you live your life. In the New Time, there can be no-one else to walk the path for you. Everything will always be based on your own efforts in life.

After an AuraTransformation™, due to its much faster vibration, the body can sometimes have difficulty in adjusting quickly to the new high-frequency tempo that the spirit consciousness is in complete control of. This is especially true for older people as well as for adults and adolescents who have been exposed to strong physical, emotional or psychological stress in their lives.

In such cases we recommend that the AuraTransformation™ is supported or followed by some kind of body-centered therapy and relaxation.

In brief, an AuraTransformation™ results in the following:

- Integration of the Crystal aura but there are still people who will have the Indigo aura integrated

- Personal development acceleration

- Better intuition and wider overview

- Intuition and decision-making strength working together, giving greater decisiveness

- More intensity about the things you are involved in and more passion about your basic ideals

- Increase in radiance and personal power of manifestation

- Diminished reaction towards resistance, strength regarding other people's views and opinions

- Greater endurance

- Inner peace, greater self-esteem and more confidence

- More true to self and own needs

- Stronger awareness of mental, emotional and physical needs therefore improved self-definition and ability to break through and set boundaries in relation to others and self

- Increased joy in life and refusal to be dictated to

by other people's hidden agendas

- No longer giving everything you have without ensuring something in return (win-win)

- Easier to show openness in relation to others without constantly having to be on guard behind the scenes

- Improved capacity for living in the moment, increased spontaneity and less rigid planning.

- People around have a strong sense of your personal viewpoint in life, often without you saying a word

- Release of old karma and focus instead on dharma, your life purpose

In some cases after an AuraTransformation™ there will be a need for an additional session to balance the energies. This is simply because the spiritual consciousness in the aura and the body may have started working overtime in order to adapt and adjust their energies to each other very quickly. This can be especially hard if you also have a busy life to lead.

It is not a prerequisite for getting a positive return from the expansion of consciousness that you remain peaceful after your AuraTransformation™ but it is recommended that you allocate time for personal reflection and self-balancing once in a while to find your way to your own inner truths so that they can be lived out in your own life.

It can sometimes come as a surprise to many aura-transformed people that after an AuraTransformation™ it is not always possible for clairvoyant people, who are able to read the astral body in the soul aura, to see that there has been a radical change in their aura and consciousness. This is because people with the soul aura and consciousness cannot always get deep-down into the consciousness, whereas spirit energy clairvoyant people can always orient themselves down into the system.

The astral clairvoyant often sees and reads the client's aura in a way that they may relate to him or herself.

If you still feel, after the AuraTransformation™, that you have karma, which some people do, it is because the themes of your karma are repeated in your dharma in the realization of your personal life purpose.

This may not immediately be seen as something positive but there is usually a very obvious reason as to why we have the life we have.

Perhaps your dharma and life purpose are to teach other people what you have learned through your life, so that you end up sharing your life experience with others, as a form of self-help.

People who are having a hard time often find it easier to take advice and help from others who have had a hard time themselves. There should certainly not be any well-educated people coming from outside trying to 'help' if they do not recognize the situation themselves from inside. That is why most 'helpers' undoubtedly have to have lived a life that forms the basis of them being able to help others.

Who needs an AuraTransformation™?

Virtually all adults who in some way feel restricted inside will benefit greatly from having an AuraTransformation™. However, an AuraTransformation™ does not cure mental illness or long-term imbalances in the mind, although it can still help to relieve symptoms.

If you also feel limited externally due to various negative influences from your situation in life, an AuraTransformation™ can help to change this situation. The AuraTransformation™ will not solve or eliminate all of your problems but by integrating a major driving force into your energy system it makes it possible to avoid inappropriate and disruptive people and/or problematic situations. Clearer boundaries are established between people, for either you like each other and want the best for each other, or else there is simply nothing more to get from the relationship.

If you would like various forms of body-related treatments to have a lasting effect, for example, then an AuraTransformation™ is clearly for you. The new aura that you will get with an Aura-Transformation™ makes it possible to hold onto all the energy and all the resources that you receive through body-related or consciousness-related treatment. Often the energy that is injected through healing, massage and similar treatments can very quickly leak out of the system again due to stress, for example but this will not happen in the same way after an AuraTransformation™. Energy can only disappear if you want it to do so.

People born before 1987

All these people can greatly benefit from an AuraTransformation™. However, not everyone is ready to give up their soul energy or is ready to acknowledge their own energy and power.
    The effect of carrying out an AuraTransformation™ in older people may prove to be somewhat limited since they usually do not seem to need a great deal of assertiveness in their lives.

Young People and Adults Born 1987-1991

These young people and adults can greatly benefit from an Aura Adjustment, or a 'mini' AuraTransformation™. This will help them come fully into place within their own energy systems and make their personal potential visible to themselves and others.

Young People Born 1992-1994

These young people are born with a predominance of Indigo energy and less soul energy, so they have great personal power of manifestation but lack protection and the ability to set boundaries for themselves and for others. They do not need a complete AuraTransformation™ but rather an Aura Adjustment.

Children and Young People Born 1995-2003

All these children are born with a pure Indigo aura and have no need for an AuraTransformation™. They will however benefit a great deal if their parents and other carers are aura-transformed and they may also enjoy getting periodic balancing or spending time with conscious Indigo and Crystal adults, who might help to accelerate their crystallization process in the aura and the body.

Children Born 2004-2008

These children are born with a mixture of the Indigo and Crystal aura and the closer to 2009 the children are born, the cleaner the Crystal aura will be and the more crystallized they will be in the body. Therefore they do not need an AuraTransformation™.

Depending on the children's upbringing and how much focus there is on consciousness development in their home and close environment, the children's combined Indigo-Crystal aura will evolve by itself and at its own pace to become a pure Crystal aura.

These children can benefit greatly from receiving physical body treatments that can help to promote their own crystallization process. Being together with other people who have Crystal energy is also good for them. A good rule of thumb is to always first prioritize the upgrading of the parents, which can happen through an AuraTransformation™ amongst other things, so that they can best assist their children in their crystallization process so that they are first 'pure' Crystal individuals and then 'pure' Crystal people.

Children Born 2009-2012

All these children are 'pure' Crystal individuals and they are characterized by their spirit being fully integrated in their body. They are crystallized in both aura and body. They have no need for an AuraTransformation™.

Children Born from 2013 Onwards

Children born from 2013 onwards do not need an AuraTransformation™ either, as they are crystallized in both aura and body and also in their network energy and therefore in the layers of consciousness that on the visible level lie beyond their aura but which, energetically, are a part of their own personal energy.

They are therefore very aware of who they associate with and the reason why they associate with those people. Right from childhood they often feel closely connected to people who they have not yet met in their physical lives, or with people with whom it might not seem logical to feel connected to. This is because they recognize the people and their energy from some other layers of consciousness in their consciousness development.

When is it not Advisable to be Aura-transformed?

It is not advisable to be aura-transformed if you are of great age physically and even more so if you are old in your mind.

If you are mentally ill, mentally unstable and/or dependent

on strong medication, you are strongly discouraged from getting an AuraTransformation™. If you are taking anti-depressants or similar medications, there must be some strong special circumstances in place to consider an AuraTransformation™ as a possible way out of depression.

If you are an alcoholic, take hallucinogenic drugs, including marijuana, or are a drug addict, it is also not recommended that you receive an AuraTransformation™.

With regard to people who smoke marijuana, it can be difficult with reasonable accuracy to predict what the outcome of their AuraTransformation™ will be, because the influence of marijuana usually sits in someone's body and mind for a very long time after consumption and has a strongly distorting effect on the person's ability to perceive clearly and coherently. This is the case even if the person concerned does not have that perception. Therefore it is not advisable to have an AuraTransformation™ if you regularly smoke marijuana.

It is also not recommended that 'spiritual seekers' become aura-transformed as yet one more in a series of many psycho-tropic experiences on their spiritual path in the search for their inner truth.

What happens during an AuraTransformation™?

Since people are very different, there are not two AuraTransformations that happen in exactly the same way. All treatment processes are individual and when two people talk about the process of their AuraTransformation™ later, they might find nothing in common other than that they have both been fitted with a new stronger protection and magnetism in their aura.

An AuraTransformation™ and an Aura Adjustment take place

through energy healing, where the Aura Mediator™ holds the client's feet throughout the whole process. However, an Aura-Transformation™ cannot be equated with normal healing, since it is, for the most part, the consciousness that is being worked on, which will subsequently be reflected in the body's reactions, since the AuraTransformation™ leads to a direct contact between the body and consciousness.

Therefore the consciousness changes immediately in terms of the emotional state, while the body often needs more time to register the new way that the energy structure is functioning.

The whole process of AuraTransformation™ usually lasts from three to four hours spread over one or two treatments, all depending on whether the treatment is combined with clairvoyance, conversation or similar. It is best for some clients that as many words as possible are connected with their personal process, while others are most comfortable reflecting on their new consciousness situation by themselves.

It is not a problem for almost any therapist to break down the old aura. It is actually quite easy. On the other hand, it requires great consciousness strength and inner balance to help build up the structure of the new aura.

In order to change the aura of another person it is necessary as a therapist to bring a quite definite broad-spectrum energy influx which all Aura Mediators have integrated during their personal training program. This is an energy that, for even the most experienced healers, will feel like having 'an entire central station' running through your head. That is why it is not an energy that you should be experimenting with just for fun.

It is crucial, as a client, to ensure that the Aura Mediator™ you consult has been trained on one of our Aura Mediator Courses, which you can read about at the end of the book. It is also very important that as a client you have a good feeling about the Aura Mediator™, because not all practitioners will feel right for the job despite their great energy powers.

There are many different types of Aura Mediators with different approaches to working with AuraTransformation™. Some express themselves in a very earthy way, while others are more intellectual in their interpretation of things. It is therefore important that as a client, when you arrange the session, you get a good, strong feeling that the chosen Aura Mediator™ can accommodate and understand your energies and ideas without problems, as well as being able to speak to you in a way that makes you feel safe with regards to the AuraTransformation™.

During the AuraTransformation process it is important that the client is as comfortable and relaxed as possible. The Aura Mediator™ always starts by scanning the client's energy system to find any blockages or old problems that need to be healed, cleansed and possibly released during the process so that the client will be ready to receive the balance body and the new aura structure with the powerful new energies.

The Aura Mediator™ will also, at this initial stage of the AuraTransformation™, get some clear indications about which areas need to be worked on with the client – for example, the neck, back, abdomen, etc., as these will be the places where the blockages are.

When the body and energy system have been examined and filled up with energy, which for many people results in a feeling of physical heaviness, warmth, tingling in the feet and hands or other places, there may be a slight sensation of pressure in the client's head. This is a sign that the client is ready to let go of the old energy bodies, which are described in more detail in the chapter *The Soul Aura*.

For most people, the energy bodies are released by themselves, giving a feeling of light-headedness, as though you had been waiting to get rid of something you no longer need. This releases the direct connection to the soul energy.

Then follows a long phase where the client unfolds their full energy potential. This is a process that most people enjoy a lot as they get a feeling that they finally have the space they need. Some people lie down or sit and enjoy the energies working in their body and mind, while others have a great need to talk about the things that pop up along the way in the form of thoughts, feelings, long-forgotten memories and visual images, etc.

These things will typically have their origin in the blockages and any other problem areas that the client may escape from forever during the transformation and/or may work with further for a while to recover their ultimate basic balance. This balance must be there in order to allow the client to receive the new energy in an optimal way. So the themes that appear often concern balance on different energy levels depending on where the client is located in his or her development.

Not everyone has the same experience during this process but the Aura Mediator™ will always get the required information for the person to interpret. The information can come in many ways - feelings, colours, lights, pictures, or perhaps through all the different forms of clairvoyance.

When the development and healing process is coming to an end, the client experiences a deep calm, or perhaps an overwhelming feeling of great joy. The reactions may vary but whatever it may be, there are always some clear signs that it is now time to gather the aura.

When the client is healed, purified and unfolded in their energy, the gathering of the new aura begins. During this process the Aura Mediator™ works in a conscious and concentrated manner, as the balance body and the new aura have to completely surround the client's body in order to function as a new protection. Many clients can feel the balance body building up around their physical body.

This can feel like being wrapped up warmly or receiving extra care and protection.

In some cases the client does not want to be 'wrapped up' again, as the sense of having infinite space and no physical boundaries during the healing process may have been so attractive that they want to remain in that state. There is, however, no turning back, as the balance body needs to be connected to the physical body so that the person can act in a positive manner here on Earth and so the limitless blissful state has to wait until the time is right for it here on Earth.

A balancing will usually start straightaway and if the situation allows, it will also be completed straightaway. If not, it is desirable to have an additional balancing around 2 or 3 weeks after the AuraTransformation™ but again, this can depend very much on the individual.

Some clients do not need for further balancing but they may need advice on body balancing treatments to follow up their AuraTransformation™.

How Quickly do you Respond to your AuraTransformation™?

Not everyone responds equally as quickly to their AuraTransformation™, nor does everyone react in the same way but overall there are a great many similarities in the response patterns that aura-transformed individuals experience both before and after their AuraTransformation™.

How quickly both the personal and energy changes take place depends however, very much on how clear and conscious you are as a person when you become aura-transformed and how much you are stuck in the old patterns of behaviour.

There can be many reasons why you might choose to get an AuraTransformation™. Some people choose to become aura-transformed for extra strength and courage for starting on a greater process of personal change in their lives. Others do the exact opposite and finish with an AuraTransformation™ as the crowning glory after they have turned everything in their lives upside down, because now they need to integrate a new and fundamental balance.

Some people might have lost their jobs or got divorced and therefore feel that major life-changes have been imposed upon them. In such cases, the AuraTransformation™ can be experienced as a lifeline so that they can finally make peace with the past. Other people simply know deep down inside that now is the time to give their aura an energy upgrade so that they can have more freedom on a consciousness level, as well as integrate a greater power for physical manifestation into their lives.

It is no wonder that some people are literally thrown into changes straight after their AuraTransformation™, while others throw themselves into change and others simply find that instead, change comes slowly creeping into their lives without them even being able to detect it clearly. People around them, however, will always notice a change in the person's personality, whether the person can detect it or not, since their energy radiance will have been radically changed following the AuraTransformation™.

The Three Aura Structures

The basic difference between the three aura structures – the old time soul aura, the Indigo aura and the Crystal aura – are as follows. The soul aura consists of materially condensed soul energy which is so compressed in its structure that it's energy is difficult to change, unless you have lived out your karma so that the energy begins to drop off all by itself, or there is a violent and boundary-crossing physical or psychological influence from outside, which makes the aura disappear or fall apart by itself from the shock.

The Indigo aura consists of a balance body, which surrounds the body and is made up of a mixture of materially condensed energy and pure spirit energy. This balance body is enclosed by an energy body consisting of very pure high-frequency spirit energy which sends spirit impulses through the balance body into the physical body.

The Crystal aura consists of a pure spirit aura equivalent in size to the Indigo aura's balance body, which sends pure high-frequency spirit impulses directly into the body. When the physical body is able to vibrate with the same high frequency as the Crystal aura, the Crystal aura and the Crystal body come together to form one large Heart chakra.

On the following pages you find descriptions and pictures of the three aura structures.

The Soul Aura

The soul aura consists of the following energy bodies and chakras:

The physical body: The shell through which spirit and soul energies are expressed.

The etheric body: The physical body's protection.

If this energy body starts falling to pieces or is broken down completely, you feel very exposed to physical and psychological influences from outside. You will often get allergies, eczema and other skin problems and you also might develop problems tolerating sunlight.

The etheric body has seven chakras, which are all a fully integrated part of the etheric body and connected to the spine.

The lower mental body: The mental library containing all learned knowledge and external learning.

In the New Time you often risk suffering from a lack of space in this library, so there may be situations where very basic knowledge is forgotten. This is because the brain is forced to discard basic knowledge or perhaps put it in the background in order to accept new knowledge and new input.

The astral body: A karmic and emotional archive of a person's past, present and future.

As you sow, so shall you reap but not always in this life.

The soul energy belongs to this energy body, where it is possible to read one's pre-determined future and actions in your past lives, as well as your emotional state at any given time.

The higher mental body:

Intuitive and spiritual energy.

It encircles the body and the other energy bodies in the aura and can be contacted through meditation and clairvoyance.

It is here that a person's unlimited consciousness potential is stored, outside the etheric body, the lower mental body and the astral body.

The seven chakras, which are an integral part of the etheric body in the soul aura, are linked together at the back:

The Root chakra:

Grounding, self-control, decisiveness and propagation.

The Hara chakra:

Physical happiness, money, sex, power, desire, the belief in being provided for eternally or anxiety about lacking things.

The Solar Plexus:

Self-esteem, patience, neurological calm, intimate relationships and family, as well as belonging together with other people without sticking to each other.

The Heart chakra:

Human love, freedom, trust, compassion, unity and the connection between the earthly and the spiritual.

The Throat chakra: Here you stand by yourself facing outwards in the form of communication, boundary setting and expression, etc.

The Third Eye: Intuition, overview, joy, transformation and spiritual insight.

The Crown chakra: Love of Everything and love of life, plus opening to the pure spirit energy in the higher mental body through a spiritual lifeline, called the silver cord or the Antah-karana.

The Soul Aura

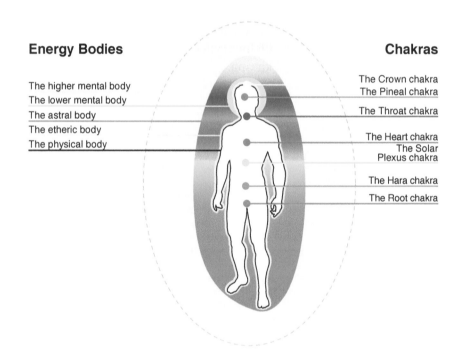

Energy Bodies

The higher mental body
The lower mental body
The astral body
The etheric body
The physical body

Chakras

The Crown chakra
The Pineal chakra

The Throat chakra

The Heart chakra
The Solar
Plexus chakra

The Hara chakra
The Root chakra

The Indigo Aura

The Indigo aura consists of the following energy bodies and chakras:

The physical body: The shell through which the spirit is expressed.

The spirit body: Intuitive and spiritual energy.

This corresponds to the higher mental body in the soul aura.

This is where an Indigo person's unlimited consciousness potential is located for full utilization, so that the body can use the information from the balance body to convert it into action.

The balance body: This acts as an interpreter between the body and the spirit body, as the body and the spirit speak completely different languages. Through the presence of the balance body they can understand each other, which leads, among other things, to a great personal power for manifestation as well as greater visibility in relation to other people.

In the balance body there are three strong energy focus points/chakras, which are connected together in the back:

The Hara chakra: Good grounding to the Earth, physical satisfaction, decisiveness, housing, money, sex, joy and family.

This contains the original qualities from the Root chakra, the Hara chakra and the Solar Plexus in the soul aura in one powerful energy focus point, which ensures a greater consistency between one's personal needs and the realization of these.

The Heart chakra: Centering, emotional balance, spiritual and earthly love combined, a sense of inner freedom, openness, compassion and honest communication from the heart.

This contains the original qualities from the Heart chakra and Throat chakra in the soul aura in one powerful energy focus point, which means that your mouth can convey what is in your heart.

The Third Eye: Mental overview, intuition, wholeness and balance, vision, continuous influx of spiritual insight and pure being.

This contains the original qualities of the Pineal chakra and the Crown chakra in the soul aura in one powerful energy focus point, which leads to greater clarity and the ability to live and be in the moment.

The Indigo Aura

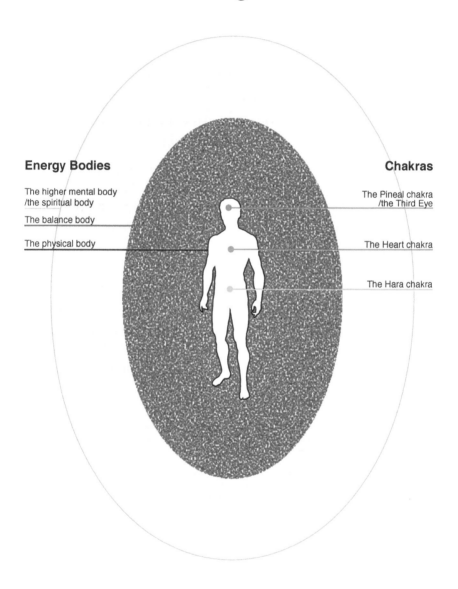

Energy Bodies

The higher mental body
/the spiritual body

The balance body

The physical body

Chakras

The Pineal chakra
/the Third Eye

The Heart chakra

The Hara chakra

The Crystal Aura

The Crystal Aura consists of the following energy bodies and a single chakra:

The physical body: The shell through which the spirit is expressed.

The aura: Also called the spiritual body, which consists of pure condensed spirit energy.

The Heart chakra: This starts by being centered around the thymus in the middle of the chest but ends up filling the whole aura and the whole body when one has completed the body crystallization process.

This represents exactly the same qualities as the Heart chakra in the Indigo aura, namely centring, emotional balance, spiritual and earthly love combined, a sense of inner freedom, openness, communication and honest communication from the heart.

The Crystal Aura

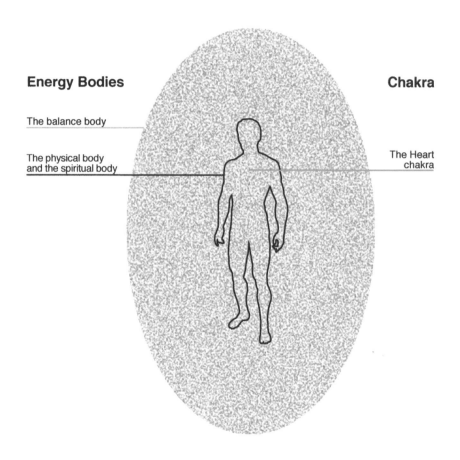

Energy Bodies

The balance body

The physical body
and the spiritual body

Chakra

The Heart
chakra

Integration of New Strong Energy Focus Points

In the Indigo aura, the seven chakras from the soul aura are combined into three extremely strong energy focus points in the body, around the Hara chakra down below, which represents physical vitality, around the Pineal chakra above, representing spiritual intuition and as a unifying whole around the Heart chakra in the centre, representing the balance that all of life is fundamentally based on.

The original qualities of the Root chakra and the Solar Plexus are thus integrated in the Hara chakra. The Throat chakra is integrated into the Heart chakra and the Crown chakra is integrated into the Pineal chakra, while the qualities of the chakras in the soul aura are preserved completely intact in the Indigo aura, although in entirely new energy constellations.

This creates a basis which allows everything to be present in each individual around the question of how to build a foundation in life where such things as housing, money, sex, joy and family belong to one and the same pool and not as was previously the case when many people were intent on having an 'exciting' life outside and a more 'moderate' life at home. On the Indigo level there is a better match between a person's needs and the fulfilment of those needs.

In the Indigo energy, it feels wrong to divide your life up so that you have your family in one place and your lover or mistress elsewhere. In this energy, the husband or wife at home is also a lover, so more of your needs can be met under the same roof. Also, the new aura and the combination of heart and throat energy in the same chakra will create a fertile ground for honesty, since communication will be a direct expression of how you feel in your heart.

With regard to the union of the energies of the two upper chakras, it almost goes without saying that intuition and spirituality become one and the same thing.

In the transition from the Indigo aura to the Crystal aura the three energy focus points are collected into a single energy with a focus on the heart, where wholeness and balance with its base in the heart energy is the key to everything.

By exclusively concentrating on how we feel in our hearts, we will actually be as centered as we possibly can. If we only experience the world with our minds and our thoughts, we often lack joy and physical satisfaction in our lives and if we experience life only with our abdomen and with our feet planted in the ground, we often lack overview and an understanding of the interconnection of things.

Wholeness, centering and balance are therefore the optimal conditions for people to be in if they want to live in accordance with the New Time energy. These conditions will all be met and satisfied by the energy structure in the new aura. However it is still possible, if you so desire, to choose great mental, emotional or operational fluctuations in your life, as you are sure to quickly regain your fundamental balance.

Expanding Awareness

The main reason that most people on this Earth need a new aura aligned with contemporary conditions and can no longer just use the old energy bodies in the aura, is that these are too strong a damper on our greatly expanding consciousness and thought universe.

As time passes, we need more space to move into with our thoughts and minds. In relation to the outside world the hard disks in many adult human's internal computers have simply become too small and old-fashioned. If you know about computers, you will know how easy it is to create, delete and re-arrange the various files in the system. If we compare this simple process to the way in which people manage their thoughts and their lives, these things are too complicated to be able to happen at the very slow tempo that is in the 'old' human energy system. This is the case for adults, because today's children have a tendency to quickly forget their miseries, unless they are actually rude, boundary-crossing or offensive by nature. Often adults remain stuck in their ills and old patterns of behaviour for years without getting out of them, though they certainly do want to get on with their lives, simply because they have the belief that certain things must have a definite sequence and that there must be a certain amount of suffering in order for things to feel right. Suffering first and then finding happiness seems to belong to the past and it does not really fit in with our modern times. In today's world – and especially in tomorrow's world – there can be no definitive life manual for the 'right' thoughts, emotions or lives. We will be helped to both understand and follow this by the energy of the New Time and the new aura.

The New Time children have come to Earth with a much greater awareness than their parents or grandparents had and this is accessible right from birth, simply in order to break with the many poor and inappropriate modes of behaviour which in the past were created in childhood only to be continued as traditions in many families. Therefore there is now hope that such things as incest and other similar types of abuse will be significantly reduced over the next twenty years, simply because there has been a tradition of twisted sexuality in many societies, without people being aware that they were doing anything wrong.

Many of the new children will know for themselves that such acts have something wrong about them – that they are an abuse of love – and so they will consciously or unconsciously try to break the extremely negative patterns without breaking contact with their families in doing so, as was done in the past. Despite everything, children still love their parents, no matter how ignorant their parents often are with regard to consciousness, humanity and love.

It is not only that the old aura is no longer in keeping with the times. It also provides too little protection for the human body, which many people have already found out to their cost. For the stronger the new energy influx to Earth becomes, the more likely people are to suffer from allergies, at the same time as suddenly not being able to tolerate the sun, which is otherwise so life-giving both for our bodies and for our planet.

On the psychological level, many people feel themselves to be more vulnerable than they did in the past. Due to the very low level of consciousness protection around the body, they can easily get a feeling that other people are more invasive than they actually are. Many people can recognize the feeling of sometimes having other people hopping right inside their abdomen when they simply greet them on the street.

Karma

People's past, present and future can be read in the astral body in the soul aura, where it expresses itself in the form of karma where they reap what they have previously sown. For thousands of years karma has controlled everyone's lives with an iron fist and perhaps many people right now are paying for some misdeeds from back in 1172 or even from the time before our era, which is quite inappropriate in the current situation!

We simply need to start afresh and say that right now we have a bigger or smaller collection of personal qualities, faults and failings and we should just see how far we can get with them and then just forget everything about what happened back in time.

This does not mean that criminals in society should suddenly be allowed to get personal rehabilitation from one day to the next, if they have not done anything to deserve it. No, they must of course get back the same thing that they are sending or have already sent out to the outside world in this life, so that justice may be done.

Karma, in the form of justice, with a much faster payback procedure than has previously been the case, is clearly preferable if the Earth's development is to accelerate rapidly and in a positive direction. Otherwise everyone will remain stuck in their own consciousness history, which they do not even have a direct means of understanding in their daily lives. It is therefore impossible to achieve personal and inner freedom before you rid yourself of your soul aura, where all your predestined history is written.

The Mental Library

The lower mental body in the soul aura is located around the head and it represents a kind of library in a given order. It contains all our knowledge and all we have learnt from outside sources right up to the present date. However since things continue to accelerate day by day and we are continually keeping track of new concepts and fresh knowledge, there is less and less space left in the library. Many people therefore end up in situations where they have forgotten parts of their basic knowledge, simply because the brain has been forced to scrap the original knowledge or move it into the background in favour of all the new input.

There is simply a lack of space in the brain, or in the consciousness if you will, so what could be better than having your intuition permanently joined to the body directly through an Aura-Transformation™ so that it can continuously remind you about everything you need to remember in your daily life both at work and at home?

Consciousness Blocking

The higher mental body, which represents the intuition and spirit within us, is located in the outer part of the soul aura.

To get in touch with your intuition you must therefore first pass through the three energy bodies in the aura – the etheric body, the astral body and the lower mental body – which is like a consciousness blocking shield between the body and the spirit energy in the higher mental body and this is experienced by some people as a much harder process than it is for others. Some people have an entire highway leading out to their spirit energy which they race down every day, while others never find their way to their spirit energy and intuition.

There are many ways to get in touch with spirit energy and meditation is perhaps one of the best known of these.

People who meditate work fully consciously, in deep calm or with soothing music, to get in touch with their spirit energy in order to find answers to many things deep within themselves and about life in general. However, for some people, the problem with meditation is that for the short period of time they are meditating they completely lose touch with their physical body and their grounding to Earth. This is because their focus withdraws completely from the body and the world around them so that their thoughts can move around exclusively in the outer part of their own consciousness. From a more practical angle it can also be enormously difficult to meditate deeply on your shopping, for example, when you are standing in the supermarket and have forgotten your shopping list as the surrounding noise can interfere with your inner concentration. So it is certainly much easier to use your intuition when it has been linked directly to your body through the new aura.

Attraction and Boundary Setting

The balance body in the Indigo aura is very strong and cannot be removed once it has arrived through an AuraTransformation™. It is possible to weaken the protection and also partly the magnetism if you decide that that is what you want.

The purpose of having the balance body attached directly to your body is that with both thought and will power you will be able to attract certain people and situations. Similarly, you will be better able to keep certain people and situations at a distance, if this is what you want and need.

In short, you will become better at setting boundaries regarding the outside world but you will also be better at opening up to new relationships and circumstances in your life, if this is on your personal wish list. Moreover, your radiance will be significantly stronger and everyone around you will be able to see how you feel about yourself. Many people who have received the new aura often experience the people around them reacting   as if they had expressed certain wishes or had spoken out about certain things, even though they have not yet opened their mouths to speak. This is because thoughts and attitudes are now located more visibly in the aura than before, making it easier to set boundaries with respect to others without needing to be really tough about it.

However, if it is necessary to be strict about setting boundaries with the people around you in order that they understand, nobody will be in any doubt about your personal opinion on the matter!

On the other hand, if you have a really bad day, which can still happen after your AuraTransformation™, without it nevertheless having a negative influence on the rest of the week, you can easily look extra tired and worn out. This is because honesty comes first, even with regard to your appearance. On the other hand, you will always be able to make a decision that now, things should be different and then, things will be different.

It is consciousness that sets the agenda for what you end up with in terms of the positive and negative experiences with your body.

Personal balance is much more pronounced when you have a Crystal aura than when you have an Indigo aura and it is thus not as easy for the people around you to interpret your mood as it is in the Indigo energy. The personal protection, magnetism and power of attraction, as well as the ability to set boundaries, are proportionately much stronger in the Crystal energy.

Intuition and Wholeness

With both the Indigo and Crystal auras, the spirit energy becomes a noticeably stronger and much more comprehensive part of your life than it was with the soul aura, since you can better relate to your thoughts, intuition and spirit energy, which are now physically present and more direct in their impact.

Through the direct connection of the spirit energy to the physical body, with the balance body as intermediary and interpreter between the spirit and body, intuition no longer appears as a remote consciousness energy which you rarely have contact with and may not even completely trust. There is therefore a shorter path from thought to action, because your thoughts and intuition, through direct contact with the body can now be acted out in life and materialized in the visible world.

Most people get a clear sense of wholeness and of having an inner and outer cooperation activated in their energy system after receiving an AuraTransformation™. If this is not the case, it is because they have previously not been used to simultaneously taking into account thoughts, feelings and their physical body.

Many people find it difficult to get deeply into themselves, both mentally and emotionally, if their bodies are running on an empty tank due to stress. Or they also might completely forget to pay attention to their bodies if they are deeply stuck in mental and emotional frustrations. If this is the case they need to tell their energy systems that it is they who are in charge now, so that the system can, if needs be, quickly start up a level of internal cooperation. After all it is we who have the power over our own thoughts and minds as well as over our physical bodies and not vice versa, unless perhaps, we are suffering from a serious illness, that we cannot control ourselves.

A balancing of a person's energy as a follow-up to the Aura-Transformation™ can therefore sometimes be necessary if their consciousness is 'playing tricks' on them. An AuraTransformation™ can turn everything in a person's life upside down, which creatures of habit may have particular difficulty in dealing with, unless, prior to their AuraTransformation™, they had a strong desire to break with their old habits and life patterns.

Once the new aura structure is fully in place – possibly with the help of a few extra balancing sessions – there are many things that you can now enjoy which before might have seemed deeply damaging to your energy system, since your consciousness perspective will have been significantly shifted.

Facts about the New Aura

There can be many different reactions to an AuraTransformation™ and there can also be many different changes after an AuraTransformation™.

Some people feel empowered the very minute they get the new aura in their energy system, as previously they may have felt trapped in a web of inexplicable inner and outer circumstances which now no longer stand in their way. Others might just need to go home and have a good think so that they can get used to the fact that they have now become lord or lady of the manor. The reaction depends on the person's basic personality, which might not have previously seen the light of day in its entirety.

The new personality is created, amongst other things, on the basis of the decisions that the person makes following their AuraTransformation™.

Living with the new aura is a very individual process for each person depending on their personal energy structure and the way that they relate to the world. Immediately after the Aura-Transformation™, many people clearly feel that something has changed inside but they may not be able to pinpoint exactly what it is. It is usually not long before they register that the outside world is behaving differently towards them relation to their new radiance. The people around us are in fact the best barometer we have that an AuraTransformation™ makes a significant difference to our personal appearance.

In the following chapters you can read about the physical and personal changes that the majority of aura-transformed people experience shortly after their AuraTransformation™. It might also take longer for these reactions to occur, quite simply because we are all different.

So if you do not respond in the ways mentioned, there is nothing wrong with you or your reaction. However, if you have any doubts, I recommend that you contact your Aura Mediator™ for help in getting clarity regarding your personal case.

Physical Changes

The Physical Body

There have so far been no people on Earth who have been able to live a long and comfortable life without their physical bodies being able to function reasonably well. Therefore, it is important to care for your body just as much as you usually care for your mind and inner being.

With the new aura you will come to feel, know and intuitively understand your body and its signals much better than before. This means that you will get more enjoyment from using your body, as well as from having sex and other physical activities.

Magnetism, power of attraction, as well as your radiance and ability to find joy in life in general, will play their part in supporting your physical well-being, so that your body will feel much more alive than was possible with the old aura.

If your body constantly feels flat, despite all your efforts to the contrary, an AuraTransformation™ can help to give faster resolution to the problem, unless the exhausted condition is caused by vitamin deficiency. The effect of various forms of physical body treatments, such as massage and reflexology, will be much stronger and seem much more relaxing and liberating for the body if you have the new aura structure rather than the old.

Health

Our bodies and our minds are constantly working together and the result of this cooperation can always be seen in our health. Therefore, one cannot expose one's mind and psyche to a whole load of unpleasant influences and expect that the body will continue to function unaffected by what has happened. That is not how the overall energy system works.

The cells in the body remember every stressful moment and every beautiful and liberating experience that they have been exposed to, as does the mind and this is true regardless of whether the incident took place more than 50 years ago or not. The body is able to recognize all possible situations that have previously caused irritation, joy or other similar emotions. That is why you can sometimes become extremely tired, for example, before you have even started to drag heavy things around. If the body has tried it before and it did not enjoy it, then that particular memory will be stored somewhere in the energy system, under the category of 'not so good experiences.'

It is therefore quite natural for the body to feel tired in advance.

If you are often ill with flu or a sore throat, etc., it is guaranteed to be not just due to the fact you forgot to take your daily vitamin pill again or that you have been sitting in a draught or in a smoky room with poor ventilation. Often it is your state of mind that is the decisive element in poor health, if you have some problems that you have to wrestle with, for example. Of course it could also be lack of exercise that makes your body weak and powerless against infection.

You should therefore continually ensure that you satisfy your interior, meaning your mind and psyche but equally remember to take care of your exterior, meaning your body and your appearance.

If your AuraTransformation™ allows you to have the consciousness capacity to integrate the Crystal energy into your aura, then often the Crystal energy will begin to make its way into the body if this has not already happened before the AuraTransformation™. This may be hard for the body and it may even take several years for that energy to find its way completely into the body, right down to the cellular level.

You can read more about the body crystallization process in my books *"The Crystal Human and the Crystallization Process Part I"* and *"Part II"*, which are sequels to this book.

In the transition to the Crystal aura, Indigo children undergo a process similar to that described but to a lesser degree. This is because they seldom have as many physical memories as adults which need to be overwritten with the new energy.

Sex and Vitality

With an AuraTransformation™, contact between the spirit and the body gradually opens up more and more, which generally leads to a larger flow of vitality through the body. Unless you have many negative and unpleasant bodily memories that you need to have processed and released after the AuraTransformation™ before you can (again) feel a genuine joy from being in touch with your own body, it is usual for sexual desire to increase in people who have had an AuraTransformation™. This is because their desire to live rises fully to the surface, which should not be misinterpreted as meaning that all people who have been aura-transformed become pure sexual animals, as the new vitality can also be used in other ways!

For many people though, the spontaneous joy of intimate physical activity emerges again from its hiding place if it has been absent for a while. In some miraculous way you no longer allow yourself to be limited by things that might previously have been a problem. After all, it is desire that is the driving force and desire does not allow itself to get slowed down by trivial external circumstances such as a stomach that is a little bit too plump or love handles on the waistline.

Personal Changes

Rediscovering your True Self

All children are born with their own unique personalities and with the potential to develop them. It is this potential that the parents help to shape in the child's first years, so the child gets a certain imprint from them. Children are also influenced by their various institutions and schools and also by playmates and neighbours, etc. They are also influenced by the surrounding environment, as well as by the moral code and any faith that prevails either at home or in the community. Also any disturbing situations in the family such as moving home or divorce, as well as stable or unstable conditions at home, will leave their mark.

Are the child's parents well-balanced people who are able to tackle many different life situations with relative calm, or are they strongly influenced by various crises in their lives? What is the atmosphere at home like? All of these things matter.

It is not actually until you are an adult that you can really break free from the imprints of the past if they feel wrong or hurtful. Few people have the strength to begin looking into who they were right from the very beginning, before the big imprints were made. It may indeed prove to be a fairly lengthy process to delete other people's tracks from your consciousness. Besides, you do not really know how you would have reacted if you had not received this imprinting.

If you have had an AuraTransformation™, things start to move quickly, so that everything that feels wrong in your energy system simply has to be removed – and then you will already be starting to find your true self and to get rid of any old and useless material, without your thoughts breaking you into little pieces.

Consciousness

For people who are not particularly aware of the importance of the imprinting they received as children and afterwards too, we need to look at the subconscious. The subconscious mind is in fact spirit energy that you do not want or are not able to have a conscious focus on and which can sometimes make someone react inappropriately in a given situation. It might be the case, for example, that the body suddenly recalls a particular incident, usually negative in nature, that the conscious memory has completely erased, resulting in the body and the natural instincts taking control of a person's behaviour. This can cause the person to respond in an inexplicable and often inappropriate way.

The subconscious might take over, for example, in situations where someone has been beaten as a child, which, as an adult he or she might have forgotten. When suddenly faced with a similar situation as an adult, the person is then able to hit out hard. In such a situation, an otherwise quiet and gentle adult can suddenly turn seriously violent with the desire to avenge the past, even though the attacker is not the same person.

For people who have an excellent knowledge of the value or influence of the imprinting that they have gained throughout their lives, we can talk about consciousness rather than the subconscious. These people generally have a good understanding of the connection between cause and effect in their lives and manage to have some control over their own behaviour.

These people are fairly aware of what they are about and they have come so far with themselves that they can begin to open up to their intuition without feeling there is any danger. There will be no skeletons suddenly tumbling out of the closet regarding past experiences.

Balance and Intuition

Balance is the main theme in almost all alternative therapies and especially so in AuraTransformation™, as the new aura is built around the notion of balance.

If someone has balance completely integrated into themselves and into their personality, it means that they can connect their intuition and their feelings in a realistic way with their expectations about things in their everyday life.

If you are in balance it is much easier to find balance in relation to the other people in your life. You will be more direct in the way you are, simply because you are no longer in the phase where you have yet to accept aspects of yourself that you did not previously wish to acknowledge. Your energy actually knows very well who you are, what you stand for and what you need and if you have balance in yourself, your consciousness will automatically search for an equal partner with whom you can share your life in a balanced way.

If you do not have balance in yourself, you will always be trying to find an overall balance through those around you. The two partners in a relationship can end up constantly acting as opposites to each other in terms of behaviour and attitudes, etc., so that energetically as a couple they will be able to meet in the middle.

Manifestation Power and Materialization Power

As your intuition is markedly strengthened after an AuraTransformation™, you will get a greater ability to sense your own personal needs and your radiance and manifestation power will strengthen to the same degree.

Having strong manifestation power is equivalent to using your personal materialization power to quickly experience some very specific things and situations in your life, without needing to manipulate others in order to do so.

This power is achieved through becoming more aware of your own needs and using your own decisiveness to act on the things in life that you really want and which may have been on your wish list for a long time

With the new aura, you will be able to send much clearer and stronger signals to the outside world than was possible with the soul aura, so that the people who can contribute positively to the fulfilment of your wishes can come and sign up for duty. The people who are able to help, in one way or another, will react much more strongly to the signals sent out than those who cannot contribute anything at all.

Once the materialization power has really been integrated into your energy system, you must then think very carefully about what you really want to commit to. Remember that people love it when one particular person entirely voluntarily puts him/herself in charge of a particular situation and takes on all the work, so that everyone else can enjoy the results. This is because the responsibility for the things that might possibly go wrong can then, in all good conscience, be placed on the pioneering person.

Therefore, if you decide to get involved in something, you must remember to set very clear boundaries with the outside world so that everyone knows where they stand.

Boundary Setting

Boundary setting is a concept that many people have a lot of difficulty with: when are you being too hard, when are you being too soft and where should the boundaries actually be?

In society, there are common standards and common boundaries. However, when you move into the personal arena, people's boundaries are very different, because of differing attitudes and differing human and physical needs.

It is important that as an individual you are clear in your mind about where your own boundaries are, so that it is possible to establish those boundaries clearly with regard to the outside world. It is also important in the family or in the workplace, for example, to come up with some common standards and limits which everyone must respect in order for things to function in an optimal way.

If you are not fully aware of where your own boundaries are, how can the people around you know when they are crossing the line? You are really doing both yourself and the people around you a favour by being clear about where you stand.

Boundary setting will definitely be an area where you will improve as an adult if you choose to have an AuraTransformation™. The energies in the new aura represent boundary setting and protection as well as the ability to master transformation and to solve problems. So if you have trouble setting boundaries in your life, the new aura can almost be seen as a necessity from the energetic point of view.

Sense of Justice

People with the new aura usually have a highly developed sense of justice. It is almost impossible for them to live with a lack of consequences if people have behaved badly. There must be and will be some concrete payback for any misdemeanour, crime, etc. It must be a tooth for a tooth and not just turning the other cheek to collect yet another blow, as this rarely puts a permanent stop to various misdeeds and evil.

In ancient times the idea was certainly that the concept of justice would help to offset all the imbalances in the world regarding the distribution of material and human goods. Soon things developed in the direction of justice having to step in as a balancing factor in connection with various assault cases so that unfortunate elements in society could get back a little of what they had themselves given out. Since very few victims are in a position to hit back hard when they have been knocked down from behind, it was instead necessary to create public punishment institutions in the form of prisons, etc.

However, there is very rarely any form of direct confrontation between criminals and their victims, besides the one that might take place in the courtroom, since criminals rarely stay long at the scene of the crime.

It can therefore be healthy for the individual offender to have a subsequent confrontation with the crime, as well as with any victims, especially if they have been caught in the act. Getting to realize the outcome of one's own behaviour – whether good or bad – can help to put many things and thoughts in a rational perspective, even though it obviously cannot undo the original action.

This same method of confrontation and accountability can be used for children and their many small tricks in everyday life, although of course justice is not just a matter of punishing people. Justice may also be used to save people.

On a personal level, people with the new aura will find that their sense of justice shows up in the form of more confrontations with their partner or with the outside world in general than they have been used to and this will continue as long as the eventual injustices continue to exist. Nothing is swept under the carpet and once the conflicts have been resolved, it can be hoped that there will be an increase in honesty and openness between the individuals concerned so that the relationship can flow more freely. It will feel very wrong to stop fighting injustice in the outside world if the unacceptable situations are not resolved or if the people concerned have not resolved their own issues. The alternative would be to no longer have these people in your life.

Sense of Freedom

A sense of freedom is an internal state which has actually nothing to do with your surroundings. If you are consistently honest with yourself and only choose to do what you feel is right, then there is no danger that this sense of freedom will disappear.

Everyone can experience periods in their life where they feel pressured to make choices or do things that they do not feel comfortable doing, or which are in direct conflict with their own inner convictions.

If this is the case, people usually do everything in their power to rapidly retrieve the sense of freedom that they had set aside because they had chosen to follow the beliefs of others rather than their own.

As a free person, you can easily agree to enter into binding agreements, relationships or work with other people, as long as you yourself have chosen the agreement, the people or the job. Then you can continue to maintain your inner sense of freedom. It is not however to be confused with the sort of independence where you only want to follow your own head without considering the people around you.

The feeling of freedom is fundamentally based on honesty and first and foremost it is you who must be honest. You must also be true to your own opinions so that you can truly both speak and stand up for yourself.

Being equipped with a new aura leads to you to becoming more honest with yourself. You will no longer be able to lie to yourself because your body will quickly sound the alarm with some very clear body language, or possibly through some illness, if you have forgotten to listen to your intuition. It will be very hard to deceive yourself for long without tangible consequences.

The new sense of freedom, which as mentioned comes from within, makes it possible for most people to dare to make their own decisions and see the truth, even if they had had difficulty doing so before. Looking the truth straight in the eye may cause some temporary psychological pain, especially if in the past you adapted yourself to the desires and needs of the people around you and did not have enough consideration for yourself.

Joy

The joy of living becomes an integral part of the life of most people after an AuraTransformation™. This is because your consciousness and thought universe are joined directly to your physical body, enabling you to live out your dreams and desires.

You have an increased appetite for life and it will feel quite wrong to know that one day you will go to the grave without first having tried many, many things! You must live life to the fullest and do all the things you want to do, in your own way and at your own pace!

Temperament

Not everyone will appreciate it if you have a bad temper and many people will not really like it if you allow yourself to get really angry with someone or something. Nevertheless, as a rule, your capacity for getting angry usually becomes stronger with the new aura than it was with the old, because you are able to cover a much greater emotional and psychological range.

On the other hand, there is no danger of you holding anything back in your own energy system which really ought to be passed on to others either in the form of praise or a huge earful. This is because honesty will have the highest priority in your life, both honesty towards yourself and towards others and when you are constantly keeping order internally, you will not have any reason to hold ill feelings towards other people because of any previous bad behaviour on their part, since all that has been wiped out.

Every small particle has been cleansed so that there is now a clean slate, which also creates the basis for good health. However, you do not have to forget all the difficult things you have been exposed to in your life, because if they were to happen again and out of some deep naivety you had deleted all the files from your internal computer concerning similar events in the past, it would perhaps be very difficult to avoid similar disappointments.

The advantage of continually coming up with feedback and reactions in relation to your surroundings as things happen in real time, is that you can be much more honest and fair to yourself with less of a need to listen to the opinions of others.

The fact that you now speak your mind means that other people get to experience your true authenticity and consequently they will not be bearing the brunt of something that happened years ago and has remained unresolved. Especially if you 'say it like it is' in the moment.

Being able to express anger does not mean that you will be a negative person. In actual fact you will be much happier with the new aura, both about yourself and about life in general. From time to time you may feel compelled to open up the verbal floodgates to tell your boss, your partner, or your teenagers your honest opinion about them. Sweet and sour need to co-exist to create an overall balance in life, as otherwise life can end up being dull, which, of course, is also an option, if that is what you want.

Radiance

A person's radiance corresponds in all its simplicity to the aura and the energy field of fine vibrating energies that surround our body and which everyone unconsciously reacts to in either a positive or negative way.

Not all auras are equally powerful and therefore do not have equally large radiance.

Radiance roughly corresponds to the power of attraction we exercise on other people, so the stronger your consciousness, particularly concerning your own needs, the stronger the corresponding radiance and power of attraction will be for getting those needs met.

Therefore, your charisma will always correspond and adapt to your immediate needs, as well as to your in the moment state of mind of consciousness. It is not without reason that many of us are at times able to detect very strong signals from other people who are looking for a partner. A person's radiance can also be dripping with lust or clearly radiate the desire for closeness with another person. This is how radiance works.

Ability to Attract

With the integration of the new aura, the balance body supplies you with an entirely new kind of magnetism relating to your thinking and your body, so that for every thought you think and for every need that your body has, you send out some quite specific signals to the world that there is something missing and that you want this need to be met by certain people – or by the world in general. The people who respond positively to your signals will then be those who can contribute constructively to the fulfilment of your needs in one way or another.

With the new aura your ability to attract will be much greater than it was with the old aura, whether this is at the top of your wish list or not. Therefore you must adjust to the fact that other people will suddenly be aware of you to a far greater extent than before, unless you deliberately choose to live a secluded life as your external signals will then, of course, match this wish.

In fact, you can almost get the surrounding world to be as you want, because you are more or less consciously responsible for sending out the signals that correspond to what you want back – radiance and attractiveness will align with this.

Magnetism and Manifestation Power

Immediately after your AuraTransformation™ it sometimes happens that many things in your life completely fall away. However, this only happens if there is a need for significant changes in one area or another that you have not wanted to look at properly before. You may also find that everything just runs completely smoothly, because the AuraTransformation™ leads to a greater sense of inner freedom that you may have been waiting for for a long time.

Receiving an AuraTransformation™ does not eliminate the problems from your life. However you will gain strength and become more discerning so that you can solve problems in a more constructive and efficient way than before and you will not get distracted or disturbed by small, insignificant things.

If you cannot do anything about something today, then why worry about it today? Your worries may just as well wait until tomorrow, while you can use today to recharge and relax in order to gather strength for solving the problem tomorrow. All too often, many people allow small and insignificant problems to affect their entire lives in a way that is completely out of proportion to the extent of the problem itself. An AuraTransformation™ will usually put a stop to this sort of mismatch.

Once you have had an AuraTransformation™, it becomes easier to distinguish small problems from large ones and to work out how much energy and how much thought you need to put into finding a solution. This is because your aura is equipped with a manifestation force and such a strong feeling for things that you will not be able to bring yourself to waste a lot of time and effort on nothing, as this is the antithesis of balance.

The new balance body, which works by being both magnetic and protective at the same time, always lets its owner know when certain people are thinking about them – be it positively or negatively. It is then up to the person to decide whether they want to get involved in the other's thoughts and life or not.

Quite simply, you decide, with your own thoughts, what you want to do. Your aura will then respond to those thoughts by sending out signals into the world that represent the views and opinions that you have arrived at. Manifestation power and magnetism always work together in the best possible way so that you can continue to attract the people, things and situations that you want.

Protection

Besides the greater magnetism and ability to attract in your charisma that you get with an AuraTransformation™, you will also be equipped with a powerful protection in relation to the outside world. This makes you better able to set boundaries in relation to others and in relation to yourself than was possible before the AuraTransformation™. This new and powerful energy protection will also, in some miraculous way, support your ability to feel confident that everything is as it should be, even though it might not look like this on the surface in everyday life.

This stronger magnetism creates the basis for you becoming able to attract the very people and things that you inwardly desire and are thinking of and the increased protection ensures that you do not jump with both feet into just any old situation.

These two things – magnetism and protection – always work hand in hand to create the best possible basic balance around each person's life. The keyword is **self-management** based on an intuitive association with the higher powers.

As the protection of the new aura is right up close to the body with no openings anywhere, it is actually possible to experience this protection as being almost physical, especially when you are feeling emotionally vulnerable. Suddenly you can experience a feeling of being totally filled up, in and around your body in an almost magical way – a feeling that can probably best be compared to growing an extremely thick elephant skin to replace an ordinary thin human skin and this is very empowering indeed.

Will

If we as humans did not have the will to want certain things we would never get anywhere. Will is our internal tool to move on from where we are at any given time and if we do not use our will, or we have no will, we will never reach our goal – external actions will not be achieved by themselves.

With the new aura, the will to live a better and more satisfying life is in many ways much stronger than it was with the old aura but if you want, you can also use your will to achieve the opposite and make things much worse.

You have to want to have a good life in order to get one, so you must actively use your will in order to achieve this.

It is totally impossible to help another human being who does not want to be helped to move on in life when their subconscious mind is at all times working against all the constructive measures that you are taking to help them start on the right path. Although you may not feel good about refraining from action in relation to family members, friends and other people who are in a bad way and seem to need help, it can be healthy to let them fend for themselves for a time, especially if they are not interested in accepting help from others.

When they have had enough of their misery and stagnation, they will start to move, with or without help from others. This does not necessarily mean that they are able to help themselves all the way just by using their own power, so it might be a good idea to give them a helping hand when they finally express their readiness.

Openness

If you do not show a general openness to the world in relation to various new ways of thinking and to other human beings and their opinions, then you cannot be very receptive as a human being. It may be difficult to acquire new knowledge and it may also seem difficult to open up to any compassionate contact externally when you may all of a sudden want some. It may result in you having an awkward way of being which rarely brings anything really positive with it.

Being open to the world and to other people does not mean that you should accept everyone else's truths as if they were your own. You can always sort through the received information and retain only that which you think you can use and trust.

If you are not open in relation to your partner, for example, or to your fellow human beings in general, you should not expect to be allowed into their personal sphere, since you are not yourself showing any willingness to let them into yours. The signals that you send out to other people and to the wider world will always come right back to you.

After an AuraTransformation™, however, a great deal changes in your personal charisma so that you can send out signals of openness, for example, if that's what you are looking for, even though openness has never been one of your personality traits. Using your will actively can take you a long way in opening to the outside world.

Honesty

Honesty is, for many people, a difficult dimension to handle, since it tends to be especially painful for those who do not want to see the truth. It may, however, be better to have a lot of pain right now instead of finding out after twenty years that your partner, children or others have failed to truthfully disclose their real views and opinions about you for all this time, just so as not to hurt your feelings.

If we can trust one another then we can go a long way using honesty which is what many people, especially young children, are constantly trying to teach their parents and other adults. This happens, for example, when a four-year kid declares out loud that he is actually not really three years old, if that is the age limit to get into the zoo for free, to the embarrassment of his parents. It may be more expensive today, as you have to pay to get into the zoo but just imagine fifteen years down the line and see what may result from even minor dishonesty.

Secrecy and concealment are created by adults to put a veil over inappropriate behaviour. All too often, this tendency rubs off on their children and they adopt concealment and other problematic behaviours right from childhood. For some families, honesty is a major issue.

With the new aura, it becomes very difficult to lie to yourself. It can actually become so bad that you get sick every time you agree to participate in something that on the deepest level does not work for you. This is because your thoughts and your body will actually cooperate to a far greater degree than previously and therefore such things as stomach ache and throat problems might well occur if you continually choose to ignore your own signals.

If, on the other hand, you are fully aware that you are embarking on something that is beyond your normal boundaries, which everyone ends up having to do every now and again, then it is possible to mobilize additional resources for the duration of the project, without running the risk of getting completely run down.
    Afterwards it may be necessary to have a good long rest or some inspiring experiences to correct the resulting imbalance. Just as you have to be honest with yourself about where your boundaries are, you also have to be honest with yourself about your personal needs.

The Urge to Help Others

The urge to help others frequently changes after AuraTrans-formation™. You no longer react automatically to unconscious cries for help from the people around you. By being clear with people that they themselves need to speak up and ask for help and advice, they are obliged to consciously choose their own paths in life. This makes it clearly visible to everyone what it is that they actually want and who they want to consult when they need help. Perhaps they would rather get advice and guidance from other people than those who offer unsolicited help.

Many adults today are far too proud to ask others for help and they often misunderstand any family members, friends or colleagues who offer it. By not asking others for help, some people maybe feel that they have more power over their own lives than they actually have but the power you have over your own life cannot be measured by the help you do or do not receive!

It can be the case that someone has been giving unsolicited 'help' to someone else and the relationship between the helper and the person needing help very quickly breaks down all by itself. Often the person with the hidden need for help finds quite a trivial reason to leave their 'helper' and instead moves towards someone better equipped to deal with things.

This is because like seeks like, until they grow apart.

Relations

Love

Love is many things but first and foremost it is a deep inner state, similar to the feeling of freedom, which one person can have for another person, animal, towards nature and every living thing.

It is therefore possible to love your partner, your family and your children, as well as your best friend, your dog, cat or parrot, or for that matter your ex-partner. It is just that you do not love them all in the same way.

You can also love the place where you live and you can love walking in the woods and so on.

The fact is that loving someone or something also gives something to you because you feel nourished and feel joy inside from being with particular people or being in the particular locations. You should remember that just because you love another person, it does not mean that this person has any right to control your life and actions. You should therefore ensure that you set your own boundaries in relationships.

You have to be realistic about your interpersonal connections, if you do not want to end up as someone's mule or servant. We all know how wonderful it is to get other people to do certain things for us instead of having to take our hands out of our pockets for ourselves – and very loving people often do far too much for the people around them without get anything back. There is often no balance in their interpersonal relationships.

With the new aura you will be able to close completely the love gates to the outside world whilst working on how to set your own external borders. It is therefore possible to say both yes and no to other people with the same good feeling inside, because you have a greater acceptance of yourself and also greater love for yourself.

Family Relationships

In a family – whether big or small – it is always a question of getting the whole to function optimally. However, the family consists of a number of individuals, who must also be accommodated in their individual needs, which, sadly, is often forgotten in the name of the whole.

After an AuraTransformation™, most adults are no longer afraid to prioritize activities with certain family members over others, as long as they know that it does not lead to outright discrimination against younger siblings or otherwise seem unfair. Not all family members, like each other equally or share the same interests or have the same needs which is something that you must come to accept – even within the family.

Just because you are in the same family, it does not mean that you absolutely have to love each other. You choose your friends for yourself throughout your life according to your desires and needs but you are born into your family and therefore have no opportunity yourself to make an informed choice. At least not while you are alive.

The dream of the perfect family where everyone does everything together is prevalent in a lot of places and it is often very damaging especially for children, as they become accustomed to living according to some standards and rules that tend to benefit the whole rather than the individual.

Maybe the children would rather sleep at their friends' house at the weekend and the father would rather go to a football match with friends than have to sit at home and eat lunch together every Sunday at one o'clock in order to maintain the family image. Instead, they could eat this kind of Sunday lunch now and again when it suits everyone. That way, everyone is happy.

Forced socialization can often create very egocentric characters, after they have escaped from the controlling embrace of the community.

Similarly the whole family does not have to go and do the shopping together every Friday evening, as it could take time from something else which is perhaps more exciting. Why can one parent not just enjoy themselves alone with the children, like many divorced parents do, without the other parent absolutely having to be present? We all contribute different things to each other through our companionship and intimacy and in this regard father and mother often share very different ways of being with their children, which are much more clearly expressed when the other parent is not present.

Most children tend to love those moments where they have a limited time with their mother or father for themselves, instead of having to always be with both parents all the time.

With the new aura you become more aware of your own needs but you also become much more aware of your partner's and your children's respective needs and so you will begin paying attention to everything in a different way from before. It may well be that things do not look so perfect on the surface when the neighbours look over the hedge but what does that matter if the family members are all happy and satisfied? At the end of day, it must be a matter of finding your own and your family's internal balance rather than accommodating other people's ideals.

Raising Children

On the subject of parenting and counselling of young people, we need to distinguish between the types of new auras that the children you are dealing with may have. You can read about the different auras in the earlier chapters *Indigo Children, Crystal Children* and *Transition Children*.

Indigo children often end up getting burnt or falling from high places before they learn that they had probably better stay away from the toaster, hot plates and burning candles and that they should not climb up higher than somewhere from where an adult can get them down again. Anything else will lead to cuts and scrapes.

Indigo youngsters learn best by testing things out for themselves and are seldom receptive to advice from parents.

The lack of respect for boundaries, so characteristic of the Indigo children, is often an issue in situations where the balance between those with whom the children live, or are around, is lacking. Indigo children cannot function in any kind of framework where balance is missing. This is the opposite of the forcibly well-mannered children of the past, who were often taught at an early age to put a good face on a bad job.

Through their own upbringing and education, many adults are accustomed to accepting shortcomings in life, particularly between people and so they do not always notice when something is wrong. Because of this, they often find their personal boundaries breached by Indigo children, who will not put up with anything.

It requires an awful lot of resources for parents who still have the old aura to deal with and educate these quick, direct and honest children and young people.

However, as soon as we as adults have integrated the new energy into our consciousness through an AuraTransformation™, it becomes much easier to keep up with children, young people and their reactions. You can even join in with their sometimes extreme and anarchic behaviour as you now know exactly where your boundaries lie.

Regarding transition children, born with a mixture of the Indigo aura and soul aura: as parents you will have to regularly switch counselling styles in order to have an educational role in relation to these young people. This is because the young people in this group often range from being totally vulnerable to being extremely aggressive in their outward appearance. They simply cannot find balance within themselves and therefore have much more difficulty in controlling their personalities than those with a fully integrated Indigo or Crystal aura. An Aura Adjustment or a minor AuraTransformation™ may therefore go a long way in solving the problem of balance for these young people.

Parents of this group of slightly out of balance young people could also consider having an AuraTransformation™ in order to be able to help and support them in the right way. This can help to reduce a possible large generation gap between the two sides.

Relationships

If, as one of the parties in a relationship, you are thinking of getting an AuraTransformation™, you can well imagine that subsequently you might think that your partner is suddenly miles behind you in his or her outlook on life, unless he or she has had an AuraTransformation™ too. This is because your approach to life can be very different depending on whether you have the old or the new aura. It is therefore better if both partners in a relationship get their new auras integrated at around the same time.

The fact is that the AuraTransformation™ will have a positive influence on your relationship because of the personal characteristics which are strengthened in each person. Honesty, openness, the feeling of love, power of attraction and so on will all be strengthened to the good of the relationship, so that you will be able to find a better way to be together.

If there are problems in the relationship, however, it will become easier for both parties to take a decision on whether the relationship should continue or not, because it will feel very hard to live your future life on the basis of something that might be a lie.

Relationships and Sex

Your sex life is probably the part of your relationship that will get the most benefit from the AuraTransformation™. This is because the new aura brings much greater magnetism to the respective parties, as long as they both have an AuraTransformation™. If they are still attracted to each other in daily life, it will feel very natural to manifest this in a pure sexual way.

Alternatively, the solution where the couple split up due to lack of sexual attraction is also possible. This is due to the fact that for most people, the sexual aspect acquires a far greater value after an AuraTransformation™ than it did before, because you can no longer choose to ignore your bodily needs and personal desires.

It happens that a lot of frustration on the sexual front thus disappears, because the intensity and energy level is increased between the partners and thus the urge of some people to seek sex outside the relationship disappears. After all, if we are adequately fed at home, the urge to eat out is reduced.

Jealousy

Jealousy is a phenomenon that mainly exists in people who are not secure enough in themselves and their own role with their partner or in other relationships. Moreover, there is often a kind of internal restriction and one-sided thinking for people even to be able to have this feeling especially if it feels uncontrollable. Nevertheless, jealousy is quite common in virtually all age groups.

If jealousy has previously been festering in the periphery of your relationships, there will be a change in this after an AuraTransformation™ similar to the changes that will appear in so many other aspects of your life. Nobody likes living with a distrustful partner. Communication, clarity and boundary setting will therefore be needed in order to bring things out into the open

Why would you want to be in a relationship where you are not entirely sure whether to trust your partner or not? If you cannot trust your partner you must re-evaluate the relationship and your own commitment and possibly even make a definite decision about ending the relationship.

In actual fact the energy structure in the new aura leads to an increased sense of one's own needs. Of course you must also practice what you preach, so if you lay down the law about fidelity, you must decide to be faithful yourself. Once you have laid down the ground rules, you will have a more solid basis for the relationship.

As a minimum requirement you should be able to trust each other in the relationship. In return, you cannot afford to keep pressing your partner to agree about everything if they feel they have made it clear where they stand and you do not agree. You have to show goodwill in relation to your partner and then hope that they can live up to all of your positive expectations. If the opposite proves to be true, then the only thing to do is to get out of the relationship as quickly as you can, whether or not it hurts deeply inside. Indeed, it may be preferable for it to be really painful for a relatively short period of your life, rather than for it to hurt throughout a long relationship.

In the Workplace

In a workplace where all or almost all of the employees have received an AuraTransformation™, the working environment and the atmosphere is often more honest than is normally possible in a workplace where this change has not occurred. This is true for management as well as the employees.

After an AuraTransformation™, people find it more difficult than usual to keep their views entirely to themselves. It's as if a wave of truth speaking rolls over the company for a long or short period where the level of commitment is increased, bringing a corresponding increase in effort and tempo. From the point view of management, this period will be excellent for dealing with various cooperation issues.

However, if there are employees who remain discontented with the working conditions, despite various initiatives and changes in a positive direction, you should not count on them staying in the job for very long after they have been aura-transformed. This may often prove to be beneficial for all parties, as there will quickly be peace in the camp, even though it may create temporary practical problems from resignations and so on.

It can therefore be beneficial for a company to invest in Aura-Transformation™ and a follow-up balancing for its employees, since the return on the investment will be huge in terms of the improvement in communication.

The basis for any cooperation will naturally change along with the personal attitudes of the employees and management, so you may need to take a fresh look at all areas of the company in order to possibly find new and different solutions for the future.

Development of
the New Time Consciousness

The Now

To be successful in your everyday and personal plans, you need to live in the now. The past is the past and unless people from your past are also part of your present, you should not pay them too much attention. It is not worth wasting resources on people who cannot feel or know that you are thinking of them and even if they sometimes sense that you are thinking of them, what use is it to if you are not actually taking the initiative to contact them?

The past and your memories are one thing, the now is something else and the future and your own desires are another thing again.

If you live your life on the basis of how things once were, or on the basis of how you think your future will be and if this is in no way connected to the present situation, you are really living an illusion and possibly even a lie. Surely it would be better to start being realistic as soon as possible.

You can easily have grand visions for your life, even if you are a realist. Living in the now gives you the power to act in relation to the things that you want to have tomorrow and for the rest of your life.

Decisiveness

Personal decisiveness and materialization power have unfortunately become a rare commodity in many places, since the will to take charge of their own lives has completely disappeared from many people's existence. Instead, it is expected that other people will build the path for you and also even do the work for you in the same way that it is expected that God will simply pave the way for you without any difficult twists and turns along the way. This is unrealistic, to say the least.

Love is the only quantity of energy that we have free control over on this Earth without having to pay for. So it will take an effort from almost all healthy adults over the world if they are to provide for themselves and their relatives.

Many people complain about politicians and the way they govern the country – and rightly so perhaps – but very few would actually want to put themselves in their place. As a politician you are permanently in the firing line and vilified by the media, no matter what you do. However, politicians have a whole team of people behind them who sit and pull various strings to accommodate different groups and agencies, etc., as best possible, while the front person attracts votes and gets either tributes or rotten tomatoes from the public.

Most voters want their slice of the pie and will take the maximum benefit from public funds and will vote for the parties that promise to leave the most cash in their pockets. When it is time to pay the bill, however, the voters are nowhere to be seen. "Why can't you just send the bill to some of those people who have too much money anyway?" "Why does it have to come out of my pocket?"

Regardless of what various politicians come up with in their election speeches, it has, as far as I know, never been God's intention that it is only the few with a lot of money who should support the many with little money. If you want to have more money and more resources – be they personal or material – your effort and input are required.

Beating other people to death because of your convictions, as happens in many places around the globe, is obviously a really bad idea, because of course there is possibility of a peaceful solution even if it sometimes does not appear that way. Only a very few active citizens engage deeply in affairs that are beyond their own everyday world, so they obviously do not fight especially hard for either their country or for the preservation of their culture, such as one sees happen in more primitive societies on Earth.

Most people are largely indifferent to the various injustices and abuse that happen around them, as long as they themselves are not affected.

Most people therefore need to have various injustices very close to home before they mount the barricades and often things have to go horribly wrong before they wake up and act.

Many people expose themselves to all sorts of unpleasant things every day through newspapers and television without trying to change the slightest thing. The problem is not theirs but their neighbour's or some other person's who has probably brought it upon themselves. How many sexual assaults on small innocent children will take place before someone wakes up and finds out how to set visible and permanent boundaries for the type of people who apparently cannot set those boundaries for themselves?

If you receive an AuraTransformation™ you will no longer be able to put up with any kind of injustice or transgression of boundaries. It needs real action and you are no longer content just to think of all the things that you could do. You get a sudden uncontrollable urge to get yourself together and do something about things where you think you can make a positive difference, so that from one day to the next you may see yourself engaged in matters that before lay way beyond your normal sphere of experience.

Thanks to the new aura, you will also get greater courage and a corresponding sense of responsibility. You can therefore choose to commit strongly to your work or other interesting projects, because it matters so much to you and you cannot help but get involved. Because of their enormous amounts of active energy, some people can at times end up totally abandoning various important relationships and circumstances in their lives because they just have to reach their goals faster than ever.

They may choose therefore to accept some consequences in their lives that others would never accept for themselves, in order to make a fortune, or whatever. These people may have paid a very high price on the personal front for their correspondingly high salary but other people would perhaps in no way envy them. Life is indeed a choice, after all!

Intuition

Intuition is our sixth sense and it actually consists of logical observations that are made without using the body's five senses – sight, hearing, smell, taste and touch.

Using your intuition means that you take into account certain elements that you have a feeling about in your otherwise rational reflections about a particular situation.

Your intuition can show itself in many different ways but most typically it is by seeing certain circumstances or events in your mind's eye before they occur. It seems as though you know in advance the specific course of events.

Intuition can also appear as an enhanced ability to detect various signals from your own body or from the surroundings as a kind of spiritual instinct that can lead you on the trail towards particular relationships and contexts. Often you just 'know' that things fit together in a different way from the one that other people are trying to convince you is the case. It is therefore very important that you listen to your own inner voice just as much as you listen to what other people say, if not more sometimes.

The impulses that contribute to your ability to detect various signals about possible relationships and that it may be appropriate to do things in a different way from how you had originally thought, actually come from the spirit energy in the new aura where intuition belongs.

In the new aura, intuition becomes much stronger than was possible in the soul aura, where this energy body is located further away from the body.

Intuition and Ethics

Intuition is the ability to move out into your own aura/awareness and orient yourself with the various human relationships and situations there. You move up to the highest floors of your own energy tower, so to speak, so you can gaze out over the landscape and get a much better human overview as a result.

What can you see from the top of the tower? Where are your nearest and dearest positioned in relation to yourself? What is it you sense the people around you are thinking, without, of course, prying into their thoughts? It is absolutely not permissible for anyone to move into another person's aura and consciousness and take a peek without authorization from the person concerned.

If your fellow human beings want information about their own personal relationships through interpretation of the aura and consciousness, they can contact a clairvoyant who can help them with this.

Our aura is our mental body and, just as with the physical body, nobody wants strangers to be able to freely obtain access to their body without asking permission first.

> If you sense when you are moving in your own conscious-
> ness that information pops up relating to other people
> and that it has nothing to do with you, then immediately
> send the thoughts back to their rightful owners or quick-
> ly move your attention onto something else.
> This is the ethically correct thing to do.

Only if you clearly feel that another person is in distress and is therefore asking for help at an unconscious level, you can then allow yourself to follow up by contacting the person directly. Tread carefully in such instances and always make sure that it is relatively easy for the other person to avoid answering your questions if they do not wish to do so, which is why a phone call is clearly preferable.

Maybe the person does not even know that they have sent out distress signals via their consciousness and aura and perhaps their own brain has not yet acknowledged how extensive their problems are.

Many people look in through other people's windows when they pass by on the street but you should not just open the door and walk right into their house without permission or hack into another person's computer just because you can, or because you are curious. That is illegal trespassing.

Maybe you can see from the street that other people are making a terrible mess in their homes and in their lives but this is just their own personal business as long as it does not adversely affect the people around them. These people themselves have to live with the mess of their everyday lives.

You may instead drop hints about whether it might soon be a good idea to clean up or even offer your help with the big clean-up which is obviously coming. So even if it is incredibly disturbing for you to look at other people's imbalances, remember that their lives belong to them.

All people are different and have different needs.

Using your Intuition

If you wish to make active use of your intuition, it is actually very easy for you to read the people around you. It is however, a prerequisite that you can relate positively to the concept of energy, especially when the outer form of things or a visible expression from the person clearly indicates how they feel and what they think or mean.

You can start by spotting some quite simple things:

How do you feel in your body when you are with other people? Do you get a headache or butterflies in your stomach, for example?

How would you feel if it were you who had a headache or butterflies in the stomach, or where you feel pressure, pain, joy and so on?

What do the things you feel tell you about how the person concerned is feeling right now?

You will usually know whether the signals in your body belong to someone else, if the signals disappear as soon as you move away from the individual.

If you only relate to what your eyes see and what your ears hear, then you often miss many details both about yourself and the other people in your life. This is not because you need to interfere in other people's personal relationships or solve their problems but it is in order to be more compassionate at work, in a relationship with a partner and in relation to children and family and so on.

It is always a good idea for you to be able to look into your own immediate situation and your possible future in your relationship and at work, etc. but on the intuitive level it is not permitted to look into other people's situations and future without their consent, if you are not yourself directly involved in the situation or in their future.

You may, for example, read the attitude of your boss and your colleagues towards you and allow yourself to sense where these people stand in relation to you, whether they like you or not and whether they are satisfied with your personal and/or professional work or not.

It does not feel good to find out too late that although neither your boss nor the others had previously expressed it clearly, they were actually dissatisfied with your work – and it would feel especially bad if there had been the possibility of doing something about it in order not to get fired.

By making active use of your intuition, you always give yourself the opportunity to change things in your own camp and hope that this improves the situation around you.

Some people are able to develop their intuition so much that they become clairvoyant, after which they can help other people to gain both human and spiritual insight, as well as answers to various personal issues.

When you have Crystal energy, there is no longer such a great difference between intuition and clairvoyance. This is due to the relatively unstructured nature of this energy. Therefore, colours, shapes, symbols, sounds, smells, images, etc. are not part of the story when Crystal people use clairvoyance. Pictures, colours and the like belong exclusively to the old time when human energies were on the soul level and were very material and compact, or decidedly low frequency. In the New Time energy where the spirit has descended into the body, you just know everything deep inside yourself without necessarily putting any definite words and pictures to it.

Overview

Having the capacity for overview is simply a question of being able to keep track of our thoughts, while being able to cope with the many impressions we receive daily from the outside world. With the new aura, it is definitely possible to have a broader overview.

If your overview appears to diminish in capacity, maybe you need to think about how much you really want to get a handle on things. Almost everything in life is a question of free will. There will always be people who thrive best when they have disorder in their lives, thoughts, house, relationships and in their everyday lives. We can see this as being what they really want for themselves.

When you have an AuraTransformation™ and move from the old aura to the new aura, it has the effect that, in a figurative sense, you get a bigger consciousness hard drive installed in your head, which leaves room for more thoughts to pass through your brain if that is what is needed. In the soul aura, consciousness had too little space to play in, so due to lack of space you had to categorize certain thoughts into being lower priority and of less importance in order to keep making space for everything new. It is therefore no wonder that we sometimes forgot even the most obvious things, because our ideas about them were either forced to the back of the memory or completely out of our head in order to make room for new things.

Having an overview is very much linked to using your intuition, because no-one is capable of being focused and attentive at all times. Even the strongest and most powerful men and women around the world need rest and sleep and since no-one can be everywhere at once, they can make use of their intuition and listen to their own inner voice – they are able to do this as much as they listen to various external advisors in everyday life. Your subconscious often captures things in the air which have not been uttered but where the impact of unspoken things is a thousand times stronger than the things in any visible agenda. If you are thus able to combine the external facts with the input you receive through your intuition, you have the best basis for having good overview in your life.

If you also have order in your everyday affairs and in your external environment, it is much easier to have overview than if everything is in disorder. So you can in good conscience buy a time manager or a calendar to keep track of your daily appointments. It can also be a good idea to write down all your wishes for the future rather than walk around with them in your head. This way you get a better overview of what you are actually striving for in life, as well as being better able to follow up on whether something needs to be changed along the way.

Meditation

It is quite usual for many adults who have had their aura changed that they stop meditating quite quickly. With the new aura, they no longer have the same need to move around in the outer part of their consciousness in order to get the energy to cope with everyday life as they had to with the old aura.

All the spirit energy that is needed is now freely available just outside the physical body. It is basically just a question of letting the energy enter the body using the power of thought, which can often be done in a few minutes, preferably in a totally relaxed atmosphere. In this way you get extra time and energy in your daily life to embark upon interesting new activities.

Consciousness Seen from Different Viewpoints

Soul Energy and Karma

It has always been said that you cannot avoid your fate. Fate is inevitable and is said to be enshrined in the soul structure of all living beings.

The concept of *karma* belongs to the soul aura structure and functions so that you always get back what you send out to the world. So you are paid what you deserve and get positive or negative feedback from the environment equal to your own attitude towards others.

The concept of karma is part of the reincarnation system in which everyone on Earth has been included as a soul individual in an overall consciousness development plan for the planet.

Each individual's soul, which corresponds to the etheric body, the lower mental body and the astral body in the soul aura, has been embodied in many different structures and lived many different lives in different eras on Earth. In fact the idea has been that every soul lives through all the possible phases of human development spread over many different lives.

The problem surrounding the concept of karma is that the feedback that you would like to get on the basis of your positive and negative actions in a given life does not always happen in this life itself. Perhaps the good and bad deeds will not be balanced up until many lives later, when it fits better into the overall plan for humanity. This could be seen as being somewhat unfair if as a modern person you have lived a life where you have been very conscious about using positive thoughts, feelings and actions in your life.

The concept of karma with its long turnaround time is simply out of date for modern people who want to live in accordance with the influx of the New Time energy.

New Time Energy and Dharma

In the New Time the concept of fate is now entirely different and far more positively oriented than it was before. Fate is no longer something inevitable and often negative in a person's life over which they have no influence.

In the New Time, fate represents each individual's very specific purpose in life, also called *dharma*, which the person is expected to fulfil, deliver and/or achieve during their lifetime on Earth.

Unlike the limited possibilities for personal fulfilment which soul people are born with, those with the Indigo and Crystal aura structure have their own free will to choose which path to walk, cycle, run, fly, swim or drive along to reach their predetermined goal and personal destination in life. A situation which requires people to have to think about and accept the consequences of their own actions.

Now that you can choose your way forward in life, there can unfortunately be delays and time lags in comparison to what you might have expected yourself, as the people around you are not always completely attuned to your new personal standpoint in life and they may therefore create some resistance.

This is where intuition comes into play as a solution to future problems concerning timing in our daily life. In future, it will be totally impossible for modern people to live without the use of intuition if they want the best possible timing for their daily transactions.

Indigo and Crystal children and the future Indigo and Crystal people will have no trouble using intuition in everyday life but for some people who want to move from the old to the New Time energy, it can feel difficult to have to choose the circumstances in their own lives as there is no specific 'path of fate' which they are expected to follow.

We could liken this to an old male lion who is suddenly let out of the zoo to roam around the Savannah. It would be very exciting for the lion to leave captivity but how on earth would he be able to hunt for food, probably without ever having done so?

The situation would just be too unfamiliar for the poor creature.

It is extremely exciting and interesting as a human being to have the freedom to travel a path in life and explore various opportunities on this path but it can also be incredibly hard if you are not 100% happy doing so.

However, it is only people with the old time soul aura structure, where everything is predetermined, who have the possibility of making a conscious choice to not have karma in their lives. New Time children are all born with the spirit-based dharma as their personal guide in life. They have no karma, so there is no unknown history from previous lives which might affect their present life in unpredictable ways.

New Time children are born *karma-free* in relation to anything that is not connected with this life.

The Energy Tower

Here follows an overview of the five dimensions of awareness that at the time of writing are possible for everyone on Earth to integrate into their own personal awareness and aura if they work consciously on their own spiritual development.

In brief, you can see the number of different chakras that people have in the soul aura, Indigo aura and Crystal aura, as well as how the elements of Earth, Air, Water and Fire function as basic energies in the five dimensions of awareness in the personal energy tower.

The dimension table corresponds in its structure to the human aura and spiritual awareness and can be compared to a sort of energy tower that each person can be in at various levels or heights.

The different heights correspond to people's spiritual capacity which, in turn, correspond to their dharma and life purpose.

Some people may look if as the tower is not very high, because they are happiest on the lower floors of the building/aura. Others thrive best at the very top, where they can enjoy the view and the overview in peace and quiet.

However, most people live their lives on the lower and middle floors of their personal energy tower, because these storeys represent the energies that the majority of the Earth's population can easily identify with.

Dimensions, Elements & Chakras of the Energy Tower

5th Dimension — The Enlightened person

28.	FIRE → Heart chakra

- Crystal aura
- 1 Heart chakra in the body and spirit at the same time
- Spiritual aura based on pure light and truth

Transition phase between Indigo and Crystal energy

27.	FIRE → Hara chakra
26.	WATER → Heart chakra
25.	AIR → Pineal chakra

The spirit takes over and the 3 chakras enlighten into one chakra. All matter and personal beliefs enlighten and dissolve. A period of emptiness and confusion without a personal standpoint in life.

4th Dimension — The Love-intelligent person

24.	WATER → Pineal chakra
23.	AIR → Heart chakra
22.	EARTH → Hara chakra

- Indigo aura
- 3 chakras relating to the spiritual body
- Less matter energy

3rd Dimension — The Love oriented person

21.	Crown chakra
20.	Pineal chakra
19.	Throat chakra
18.	Heart chakra	WATER
17.	Solar Plexus
16.	Hara chakra
15.	Root chakra

- The old time soul aura
- 7 chakras relating to the astral body
- Emotionally controlled love energy
- Matter energy

2nd Dimension — The Balance oriented person

14.	Crown chakra
13.	Pineal chakra
12.	Throat chakra
11.	Heart chakra	AIR
10.	Solar Plexus
9.	Hara chakra
8.	Root chakra

- The old time soul aura
- 7 chakras relating to the lower mental body
- Mentally controlled balance energy
- High matter energy

1st Dimension — The Earthly oriented person

7.	Crown chakra
6.	Pineal chakra
5.	Throat chakra
4.	Heart chakra	EARTH
3.	Solar Plexus
2.	Hara chakra
1.	Root chakra

- The old time soul aura
- 7 chakras relating to the etheric body
- Survival oriented body and earth connection
- Extreme matter energy

Here is a brief description of the types of people who belong in each of the five dimensions of awareness:

First Dimension People

First dimension people belong mainly to the more primitive societies around the Earth but you can also easily run across them in more established communities, where they appear as earthy people thinking only about themselves and their possessions.

First dimension people only show compassion if it pays off financially or if there are other benefits associated with it. These are people who are focused on pure survival and only relate to the visible or 'rational' factors in life.

They are used to fighting for things and they will willingly wear themselves half to death to get extra money and material goods and they are not afraid to use their bodies to achieve their goals.

First dimension people have the old time aura and are extremely material and compact in their energy. They represent the heavy Earth element and have seven chakras that are all related to the etheric body in the aura. When the bodily protection in the etheric body disappears when the fifth dimension Crystal energies penetrate to the Earth, these humans will probably get sick and die unless they choose to follow the general evolution into the New Time.

Second Dimension People

Second dimension people are the people who are the most numerous on Earth. They are found in all established societies where they usually live quite ordinary lives, which they can manage themselves and have arranged as best as possible in the given circumstances.

Second dimension people believe in not rocking the boat and in keeping up appearances, so if there is anything wrong anywhere, it will only rarely be brought to light and only in a very safe environment, when they are intoxicated or influenced in other ways. In this dimension, you will hear the truth from children and people who are drunk.

These are people who are very focused on adapting 'correctly' to their everyday life in terms of relationships, family, job and housing and they know that things cost money. When something goes one way, something must also go the other way in order to create balance. They are interested in money and in what can be bought for money, i.e. material goods and they understand their own value so they do not get cheated at work or elsewhere.

Second dimension people have the old time soul aura and are less material in their energy than first dimension people. They represent the lighter Air element and have seven chakras, which are all related to the lower mental body in the soul aura. These are people who consider themselves to have found their mental viewpoint in life and do not intend to change it unless the pay is good or it is trendy to do so. Therefore these people only go voluntarily towards the fifth dimension Crystal energy if they receive a tangible benefit from it in one way or another. It could be that they become more popular or earn more money, etc. Otherwise they would prefer to withdraw from society to live peacefully in their familiar surroundings.

Second dimension people have simultaneous mastery over both the first and second dimensions in the tower.

Third Dimension People

Third dimension people are found in spiritual and religious circles, as well as around alternative therapies and ways of life. They often act as counsellors, psychologists, therapists, emergency workers, etc. for all kinds of people in different kinds of societies in the world.

Third dimension people are 'pure love' people who are able to completely sacrifice themselves for the world, their faith, or other people. They are emotion-driven and emotional, which can hurt them in their work and in their dealings with other people, as with their compassionate minds they risk getting far too involved in other people's lives and problems.

Third dimension people may find it difficult to live their lives based on their own desires and needs. They often base their lives on helping others or on having totally unrealistic dreams. In some cases, they develop extreme dependence on specific individuals in their lives.

Third dimension people have the old time soul aura but are much less material in their energies than first and second dimension people. They represent the liquid Water element and have seven chakras which are all related to the astral body in the soul aura. Third dimension people are very focused on the purpose of their lives and often have a very strong urge to find the way to their true selves.

It almost goes without saying that third dimension people have better mastered their own dimension than the other two dimensions present in their energy tower but they often fall directly down into the first dimension with a focus on survival if they do not have anything important to live for in a given period.

The second dimension is generally far too boring for them and so they prefer the large human variations that life in alternating first and third dimensions has to offer.

Fourth Dimension People

Fourth dimension people have an Indigo aura which contains far less material energy than the very material old time aura. The characteristic of the Indigo aura, as we have already seen, is that the body is in direct contact with the spirit body which is located in the aura around the balance body.

Fourth dimension people are people who have an intelligence about love, whose energies represent a strong combination of the Earth, Air and Water energies from the first, second and third dimensions, which have now been raised to a much higher-frequency level where the energies are represented in three strong energy focus points - the Hara chakra, Heart chakra and Pineal chakra.

The characteristics of fourth dimension people are described in the main chapter *Indigo Children*.

Fifth Dimension People

Fifth dimension people have a Crystal aura, consisting of pure Fire and spirit energy. When they become fully crystallized in the body, the body begins to consist of the same energy as the aura but in a more physically compressed form.

In order to access the Crystal energy in the fifth dimension, Indigo people must pass through a long and difficult transition period where the spirit takes full control of their lives and all their materiality and old personal beliefs are revealed and dissolved.

This is a period of great confusion, a feeling of emptiness and lack of a personal reference point in life, where many things change in importance and everything is turned completely upside down. Energy moves from the top down through the chakras in its attempts to turn the three chakras into one, and the elements change character along the way so that the chakras can lose their original qualities.

The Pineal chakra has its intuitive Water energy replaced by Air energy, so it feels like you become totally blank in the head from one moment to the next and this experience continues until the fifth dimension's state of consciousness arrives permanently.

The Heart chakra, which in the Indigo energy represented human spaciousness and generosity due to the presence of Air energy, flows, from one moment to the next, with Water energy, so that your world and your emotions totally break down. Suddenly, you are no longer in control of how you feel and what you feel, so you might just as well let your emotions run free once and for all so that the heart energy can have room to grow.

Last but not least, the Hara chakra's Earth energy, which represented reason and grounding in life, is replaced with Fire energy, which gives a boost to your sexuality and desires. When the fire is burning and taking control of the system, you are almost pressured from inside to do the things in life that you really want to do.

The characteristics of fifth dimension people are described in the main chapter *Crystal Children*.

Fourth and especially fifth dimension people are always able to travel up and down in the elevator of their own energy tower, so they can meet friends, family members, colleagues, clients and others who may be on very different levels from them.

However, it is one thing to have the ability to be constantly flexible with your consciousness. Another thing is whether you feel good doing it, or not.

It is important that each individual precisely identifies the energy level in their own energy tower where they can thrive rather than having to travel up and down in the elevator all the time to meet other people's energies.

Flexibility is a nice quality to have but it is best not to overuse it, unless it is included as a specific link in the realization of your life purpose. This is because it always takes time and effort to return to your own level when you have been travelling up and down in the energy elevator and you risk having problems finding inner peace.

Rise in Consciousness

Everything in life is measured by people's own efforts and abilities, so for both children and adults in the future there will be a tendency to divide them into two general groups – *those who have the will and/or abilities versus those that do **not** have the will and/or abilities* – simply because people will no longer be able to lie to either themselves or others with regard to their personal qualifications and commitment in various areas.

Fortunately, there are no people on this planet who are totally devoid of all abilities, so everyone still has the chance of being able to move their consciousness in an upward direction at different speeds, so that the group of people who lack willpower and abilities will gradually diminish.

Previously there was a very large middle group of people who followed each other fairly closely in education and on the labour market and only very small groups at the top and bottom who stood out from the crowd at school and in the workplace.

This will now change appreciably, so it will be obvious to every-one who has the will to move forward in life in their chosen area and who has neither the desire nor the will.

Some people will aspire to heaven, while others will prefer to relax in their own homes for the rest of their lives. One definite fact is that more and more strongly-spirited people will come to Earth in the form of the New Time children, who will all be looking for a more general truth in life. Focus, therefore, will shift away from the notion of survival as the controlling element.

Indigo and Crystal children have much stronger resilience in all areas than their parents and previous generations, making them able to live life more intensely, without this affecting their physique and psyche. In actual fact, New Time children have only one thing to take into account in life in order to ensure their own wellbeing and that is that they must always remain at the consciousness level in their personal energy tower, where they naturally belong. If they do not do this, internal imbalances can occur which will quickly spread to their external lives and cause stress, poor health and/or lack of balance in relation to other people.

Parents need to take the elevator up in their own personal energy towers in order to meet the children where they naturally belong. This would be extremely stimulating for their own per-sonal awareness and inner balance.

Of course it is possible for children to move down in frequency to meet the older generation on their home turf but it is not really healthy for the children's inner balance to do this too often. This is like Hamish and Janet coming home on a visit to their Scottish village after studying or working for years in Paris, London or New York. Everything at home seems very small, there are few development opportunities for young people who naturally want to follow the latest trends in society. It feels in many ways as if the roof is too low and that Hamish and Janet are hitting their heads against it.

The energies at home seem almost frozen in comparison with the pulse beating in those cities and if young people feel that time has stopped when they visit their childhood homes they often end up staying away altogether. Parents must therefore take a trip to the big city, so that they can go to a museum, a café or the theatre and have some exciting adventures together with their children.

It is not always because young people do not want to be with their parents that they stay away from home. It may simply be because they are bored or no longer feel at home in the energies lower down in the energy tower.

If parents choose to have their consciousness transformed and expanded, they automatically rise to the fourth or fifth dimension and then they will even find it interesting to visit the young people in the city with its many opportunities for development, rather than the children coming home to them.

You could say that the adults rise in their consciousness, which means that they increase in frequency in their own energy towers, so that they better match the influx of New Time energy. As a bonus, young people often feel more inclined to visit their parents, because they are able to recognize their own fourth and fifth dimension energies and therefore feel at home.

The goal for the majority of people on this Earth is to grow optimally in frequency, so that the focus can be on holistic and individual balance in the fifth dimension rather than on survival in the first dimension. There is, therefore, a personal life plan for everyone, so that awareness can reach all corners of the planet as the years pass. That is precisely why every child on Earth in the years around the millennium change is born with the New Time Indigo and Crystal energy fully integrated into their auras from birth. They are thus optimally equipped to shape the world in a positive way when, at some time in the future, their parents hand over the governance of the various communities around the Earth to them.

Fall in Consciousness

It may exceptionally be the case that people undergo a drop in their energies instead of the obligatory rise, which is the goal for most people. This is especially true for people who have extremely high frequency energies embedded in their consciousness and have the feeling that they have never landed properly in their body. This is a reality for many adults whose energies have previously not been very visible to their fellow humans. This is because previously it was not possible for people on Earth to see the upper floors of the people whose energy towers were so high that they reached all the way to heaven.

The upper floors of the energy tower have simply been covered by a mass of clouds, which is why other people have not been able to clearly orient themselves as to the scale of the consciousness of these people and the people themselves have not always been able to explain why this is either.

It is characteristic of high-frequency adults who do not even know that they belong at the top of the energy tower and still surround themselves with the old time aura structure that they are often very spiritual by nature and lack proper grounding with the Earth. Some of them even have direct contact with spiritual guides on various levels of awareness in other dimensions who they interact with daily. However, this often actually turns out to be contact with their own energy on the highest floors of their own energy tower.

This is because people with the soul aura are more likely to listen to other people and creatures from the outside rather than listening to their own inner voice. They feel it liberating to think that it is great spiritual beings who are speaking to them from the heights.

High-frequency people with the soul aura often have this kind of experience, until the day the upper floors of the tower are integrated into being their very own energies.

Of course it is possible to have physical contact with deceased persons and alien beings, as many clairvoyants have but it is often a contact that takes place in the more earthy energies and thus at the bottom of the energy tower as this is the only place you can communicate with something or someone that has a partially physically condensed form.

The Global Development

Fourth and fifth dimension today and sixth dimension tomorrow, or when?

You can read about the sixth dimension in my books *"The Crystal Human and the Crystallization Process Part I"* and *"Part II"*, which are sequels to this book.
What will come next after all of this? How much can we humans continue to expand our consciousness and what must we be prepared to accommodate in our energy systems in the future? Why is this development on-going and when will it stop?

There are countless questions and there are guaranteed to be a countless number of sensible and scientifically illuminated explanations and answers to all of them, which may be highly relevant in some contexts. On a personal note, I think that there is plenty for us to concentrate on in this life with the personal and consciousness-related challenges and opportunities that we have. In the future, our children, grandchildren and great grandchildren and so on will be just as willing, I hope, to live their lives in the best possible way with the opportunities that present themselves at the time, in just the same way as we have done in our time. Each age has its own charm and its own challenges.

Whatever speed of consciousness we personally want to move at, there are always some general factors that apply and that we cannot avoid in our life choices. That is why there are not the same opportunities to expand our human awareness optimally in all places on the planet.

For example, in the period around the year 2000, Scandinavia had a pure influx of fifth dimension spirit energy and is therefore very advanced when it comes to knowledge about combining spiritual and bodily energy.

In earlier epochs, the Earth experienced similar large openings for an influx of consciousness in such places as Egypt, Greece and Peru.

The Difference between Spirit and Matter

Matter represents stagnation and lack of movement in various forms and *spirit* represents eternal movement.

Comparing the energy structure of the three different aura structures – the soul aura, the Indigo aura and the Crystal aura – there is very little movement or flexibility in the soul aura, more movement and flexibility in the Indigo aura and a great deal of movement and flexibility in the Crystal aura. Therefore, children and adults of the future will be far more mobile in their energy structure than previous generations. Not however in the sense that everything will run out of control around the world and that the various communities will lose their basic stable structures. Instead, future people will be much more simple in their way of living and in fulfilling their personal needs. All unnecessary items in life such as people who do not want to do their best, old furniture, old luggage and the like will simply not be chosen if they hinder Crystal people in their personal development.

Future people will work with all their simplicity to finally get spirit into matter, so that life can flow more easily. Crystal people react strongly to any obstacles on their path in the form of inappropriate resistance. They are always best when there is free passage for their thoughts and feelings and for their way of being.

The 'material' is not only furniture, clothes and money. It is just as much the thoughts and emotions of both a positive and negative character that everyone sends out in relation to one another.

One person's thoughts can block another person from easily realising their desires and goals in life. Similarly, other people's positive thoughts can help to support the realization of a person's good ideas.

The reason that the spirit in tomorrow's Crystal aura structure is located inside the body rather than being outside of the balance body in the aura, is that in this way, spiritual expression can come to shine fully through the most material part of us, which is our body.

This is the most obvious way to raise people's heavy energy frequencies.

If the materiality moved up into the spirit as part of the development of the human consciousness instead of moving into the body as now, then everyone would lose their grounding to the Earth or they would die because they would no longer have any place in which to connect their spirit energy here on Earth.

If you lose touch with your body, which is home to a person's heaviest material energy on the planet, then it is no longer possible to live an earthly life with the visibility that is needed for people to be able to see each other every day. Then all the different spiritual beings from all the different dimensions of consciousness which inhabit the bodies of people on Earth would become invisible to each other and they would not be able to communicate with each other at the interpersonal level through their bodies.

If that were the case, you would suddenly see first dimension people hanging in the air close to the Earth, where they would gather in large flocks and growl at one another. Second dimension people would hang a little more spread apart further up in the air and communicate with each other in a lighter tone, while the third dimension people would float up and down and in and out between each other's energies even further out in the atmosphere, where they would suck all foreign impressions towards them as though it were pure nectar.

Fourth and fifth dimension people would be on the same level very close to Earth that the first dimension people are on but all fourth dimension people would appear with a much stronger force and greater magnetism around them than the first to third dimension people.

Fifth dimension people would stand with a very strong spiritual focus around their Heart chakra, so the surroundings would be totally enlightened and perhaps even blinded by their strong light.

It is a fact that spirit beings from different dimensions of consciousness would have infinite difficulty communicating with each other on an equal level, which the body helps them to do in the visible world. In the visible world everyone looks almost identical in their body structure, which corresponds to their heaviest materiality, although they differ widely in their spiritual consciousness structure behind the scenes.

On Earth, the physical body functions as a common denominator - a reference point which is comprehensible to all.

There are even people who, after their deaths, choose to keep their spiritual consciousness in close contact with the Earth, although they no longer have a body. This is either because they value the materiality of this planet, or because they feel attached to particular places or people, or simply because they are not able to commit themselves to the pure spirit energy further out in the atmosphere.

These creatures, who can really no longer be called people because they do not have a body through which to express themselves, will in some cases be helped further in their overall non-terrestrial development by an astral clairvoyant, who can navigate among the relations on the non-physical Earth level.

The right side of the physical body corresponds to a person's physical power of action in the material realm. This side is usually strongest in men.

The left side corresponds to the spiritually conscious and more intuitive energy. This side is usually strongest in women.

When the transitional period between the fourth and fifth dimension is opened up completely for the influx of pure spirit energy and intuition, this can run the risk of the brain reacting very violently with a great deal of pain as a possible consequence. Your head is simply about to come off.

It is in fact deeply chaotic for the brain to allow a mass of spiritual light into it all at once, because then the structure and materiality must surrender itself to some completely unstructured states, which it did not know about at all.

You can be extremely tired and your brain may feel like it is completely out of service: it takes a lot of adaptation for the body to completely integrate the very high frequency and unstructured spirit energy into its material stronghold, as spirit and matter are basically two incompatible elements which miraculously manage to fuse together at this time and provide some very exciting opportunities for development.

For example, clairvoyance based on images, colours and shapes, etc., belongs to the lower material spheres in the energy tower and it is very difficult to maintain such a capacity in the spiritual spheres at the top of the tower.

In the spirit you know everything deep inside yourself without being needing to put words or pictures on any of it, whereas pictures and other visible factors have a far greater value in the heaviest material sphere closest to the Earth, because they may help to illustrate a spiritual state in a very concrete way.

In the New Time energy, everything happens in a much easier way than before as long as you can adjust your system to living and working in these new energies. If you can relate realistically to life and the energies around you, then all your needs will be continually met and satisfied as they arise.

You will no longer have a need to attract a lot of material things into your life just to own and wear them. There will be a new lightness in the way people live, where material, low-frequency things are not so important in life, unless they are helping to support the well-being of the spirit in the body.

Everything always has a greater meaning and there is a specific purpose for the things, people and states that we attract into our lives.

If the spirit is present in a dancer, for example, they will seem incredibly light and graceful in their dance.

If materiality is present, the dancer will appear intense and concentrated and it will be fully visible to everyone that the dancer has been training really hard to master their bodily expression.

When two people talk together and they show openness towards each other, spirit energy is immediately present, because there is free passage in and no impediment to their mutual communication.

On the other hand, if they are dismissive of each other, then black clouds will often hang in the air between them, shaped by their negative thoughts about each other. These thoughts appear as a blocking material energy that inhibits communication between the two sides and only allows communication in a closed-minded way.

This is always felt by other people through their intuition or subconscious.

Although people may not perceive the various positive and negative energies between each other with their eyes and ears, their minds will always catch all the signals and energies that move around them. Through conscious use of intuition and the body's instincts, they can clearly get a sense of how far they are able to come in communication with another person and how much their counterpart is positively or negatively inclined towards them. If there is space and spirit energy in the radiance around the person, they are generally positively inclined but if it is very closed and material around the person, they are usually negatively inclined or unreceptive, so that you may have to put your case in a particularly convincing way. It therefore demands more resources to speak with someone who is material and closed than with someone who is spiritually open.

Use your Consciousness Constructively

Magical Powers

Everyone has the ability to be able to change their own life situation, as long as they have the will for positive change within themselves. So even though many people cannot imagine that it might be possible, perfectly 'ordinary' people may be able to work with magic in their daily lives. This is particularly the case for all those who have the new aura around them, because magic in all its simplicity is conscious use of energy.

Using Energy and Magic in Daily Life

Working consciously with magic in daily life is a powerful way to create certain conditions for yourself.

Magic is easy to work with as long as you realize beforehand how big a materialization power and manifestation power is associated with the energy you send out. You should therefore remember to use energy wisely and responsibly, especially in relation to other people, since it is in no way intended that people should be sent into a black hole by being totally transformed through magic.

Working with magic, or energy if you prefer, may only have a positive purpose, which is balance. Often you end up having to sort out the mess yourself if the energy has been used in an inappropriate manner in relation to people close to you and you have not thought hard enough about your energy manifestations.

The art of using magic is to identify the need and then to find which type of energy is required. When you work with magic, it is only the thought that counts. Therefore you do not need to see either the energy or the process in your mind's eye in order for things to work in practice.

You may try to influence all situations – personal as well as global – with positive energy from your position on the sidelines. There will be a result, although it may well take some time before anything happens, depending on the receptiveness of the individuals involved regarding energy.

For example, if you hear about unacceptable situations and experiences in the world that offend your sense of justice, it will do good to pour transformative energy onto the events in order to help provide a more rapid solution to the problems.

Energy cannot do everything by itself though, which is why there will be a permanent need for concrete work and financial assistance to crisis zones around the globe that are unable to fend for themselves.

Magical Recipes

One of the arts of using magic lies in being energetically persistent and also striking at precisely the time when the 'adversary' thinks that you have given up and are at your weakest. The less attention and energy you give your potential opponents, the more of their own energy they have to use in their fight against you.

If other people cross your boundaries in one way or another, you can see for yourself that the boundary-crossing people themselves are burned with a pure flame, as if they had been burned to ashes. There must not be a single part of the person's energy that escapes the flames of truth. In this way the proper context is illuminated for all parties involved, including the boundary-crossing people themselves.

You can also see for yourself that all the resistance that other people send or have sent in your direction changes character from being negative and dark to being a positive, bright and joyous energy which benefits you.

Alternatively you can use your thought power to send resistance back to the sender, so that they have to deal with the negative energy in their own system themselves.

If you want to work consciously with energy on a daily basis, I recommend you read my husband's and my little book *"The Little Energy Guide 1"*, which contains lots of information about this exciting topic in a very concise form.

Pure Love

If it feels difficult to know when to use boundary-setting energy and when to use transformative energy, because you may not be entirely clear yourself about your position regarding certain situations and people, you can instead send out pure love to the situation, person or group. The energy will then be distributed in the best possible way, without you as the energy provider knowing exactly what is being triggered by the boundary-setting and transformative impulses.

Pure love is quite simply magic – especially when that magic takes place between people who really love each other – and if other people have trouble dealing with kindness and good vibrations, they will do anything to avoid you and your positive energy.

Wishes

Many people send out a mass of wishes to heaven every day, hoping that these wishes will come true as soon as possible.

One minute they want a new car and the next minute they want a new partner or a new lawnmower. The fact is that every day the wishing well is filled with more and more coins, all of which have wishes attached of various sizes.

Everyone carries around a mass of wishes for themselves, for other people and for the whole, so that the higher powers are never short of tasks they need to carry out.

However, if you want to have some very specific wishes fulfilled, it may be necessary to prioritize your wish list, so that the less pressing desires take a back seat. Also you cannot just wish for whatever you fancy without considering the consequences, as some of your wishes could collide with each other if they are fulfilled simultaneously.

Wherever possible you should seek to precisely define your wishes, if you don't want all of them to end up as pure wishful thinking and disappear into the mists of the universe. You should also remember that your wishes and thoughts about life are not always related to yourself alone but that they very often involve other people to a greater or lesser degree. It is therefore a requirement for getting your wishes fulfilled that the people involved go along with your different ideas and it is here that your many wishes should begin to form an orderly queue so that it may take very long time for them to be fulfilled.

The people around you are perhaps not always willing to participate in your life plans in the way that you would like, or they may need some time for reflection before getting involved. It can also happen that they might at first be happy with the idea but then shortly afterwards start making demands and expressing wishes that go in completely the opposite direction from your original plan. In that case, you may have to either adapt your wishes and plans, or find some extra patience. It can take a particularly long time if the result is left solely in the hands of the higher powers, as they need extra time to galvanize the various people involved, by working through their intuition.

It is also clearly advantageous if you coordinate your own desires with those of your partner for example, so that he/she does not dream of manifesting a fast little sports car, while you are aiming for a people carrier which seats eight children and a dog.

You will get the furthest with cooperation and by relating to things in a realistic way!

If you want some very specific things, or you want money to realize certain concrete goals, it is best to simply send the pure desire directly to the highest power, which many call God's power, without any kind of conditions as to how the desire is to be fulfilled. This way you ensure a more optimal solution to the problem than you probably would get if you had to manage the process yourself.

It is thus all about having complete confidence in the higher powers and their actions, since they have a much better overview of everything than we do, especially down here on Earth, even though we are potentially just as intuitive as they are.

Be your own Magician – other People are too!

If you feel bad about working with magic because it feels wrong to penetrate other people's energy reserves to possibly move them in a direction against their own will, then you should of course avoid sending these thoughts and energy manifestations out into the atmosphere. On the other hand you should think about the fact that all people always have the very same energy rights and opportunities to set boundaries and to transform things as you have yourself. In truth, who knows when and how other people are internally trying to affect the whole and/or one's personal situation with their conscious or unconscious thoughts, so you might just as well try to bring the most possible positive energy to any situation.

Masculine and Feminine Energy

Balancing with AuraTransformation™

The balancing that takes place after an AuraTransformation™ covers all aspects of a person's mental, emotional and physical state. However, in a few cases where various imbalances have been leaving deep marks on the cell structure over many years, the body needs to be subsequently treated by a physical therapist.

When carrying out the balancing, the Aura Mediator™ actually only focuses on balancing the masculine and feminine energies in the client's energy system, as these two energies are catalysts for all other energies and states in life and in consciousness. This is because life consists primarily of two main opposing energies – the masculine and the feminine – which need to be aligned and balanced against each other. It should not be thought that during this balancing the Aura Mediator™ spends the whole time observing what is currently happening on the masculine and the feminine front, since the energies often support each other in the balancing process without having a special focus on one side or the other.

Incorrect Perceptions of Masculine and Feminine Energy

Many people mistakenly believe that the masculine energies relate to male features and the feminine energies relate to female features but this is not the case at all. The energies are in no way gender-specific and therefore they do not have the slightest influence on our human body structure and physical appearance. The masculine and feminine energies relate instead to our aura and energy field and are therefore magnetically conditioned. This is why they affect our radiance and behaviour, where they very much influence our personal power of attraction with regard to the people around us. Our personal power of attraction, in contrast to our appearance, is something that can be changed either via an AuraTransformation™ or by working consciously with the psyche.

The Egg and the Sperm

The concepts of feminine and masculine are actually best explained by looking at the creation process of the egg and the sperm, where it is possible to create both sexes out of the union between the two. This happens even if from an energetic point of view the egg represents the feminine energy and the sperm represents the masculine energy.

Among other things, the masculine energy is characterized by the tremendous speed at which sperm have to mobilize in order to compete in the big race towards the egg, as millions of sperm cells set off in the same direction at the same time.

Also the sperm must be able to adapt to the extremely long waiting time that can elapse before the egg is willing to accept one, or sometimes two or more, sperm cells into the warmth at the same time.

Countless times the different sperm cells have knocked in vain on the egg's door like luckless suitors but since the time it accepts them is extremely limited, it is completely cold and uninterested if the sperm cells arrive out of season. When the egg is ready for action, it must announce this loud and clear, so no-one is in any doubt. However, it is not all suitors who are accepted, since the egg is very selective in its choice of partner – or partners.

Inner and Outer Energy

From a more global and magnetic context, the feminine energy represents, on the spiritual level, the inner core of pure knowledge and insight, inner peace, overview, calm, the ability to hold together the forces and the will to steadfastly stand firm in one's views to the very last. It simply does not give up, unless it wishes to itself.

The masculine energy on the other hand represents the outer energy corresponding to the semi-permeable membrane which is found around the nucleus itself. The masculine energy seeks to defend the feminine energy and is therefore obliged to hold an extra-large power of action and an ability to adapt to its surroundings and be in perpetual motion so as to be always at the forefront of any events that may arise.

It is not acceptable for it to have a lack of feeling about things, as it could then in a weak moment be at risk of being overrun by the enemy, so that the kernel in the form of the pure feminine energy will be totally unprotected and thus be accessible to all. This includes those who do not know how to manage their energy and knowledge in a responsible way.

Masculine and Sociable

Now, the masculine energy does not only use its life to defend the feminine energy. The masculine energy is also extremely sociable. It is by nature extremely curious and has a great desire and need to be constantly setting new things in motion. It also loves to be able to move around in the big wide world in the hope of using its flexible and changeable mind to convey the knowledge of the feminine energy to others. This is something that the feminine energy in its purest form cannot do and so from this the masculine energy of course has a lot of exciting experiences and contacts, which the feminine energy never can have.

The Feminine Needs the Masculine

The feminine energy is totally unable to obtain any meaning for its life and for the many thoughts that it has every day if it does not have the masculine energy to pave the way for it out in the big wide world, so that all of its accumulated knowledge can be transformed into concrete action.

If the feminine and masculine energies are united into one single force in one and the same person, which will happen with an AuraTransformation™ and the subsequent balancing, then your life will really be going places. There will then be nothing that you cannot manage yourself, if need be, or which you cannot find a solution for with assistance from the outside world, which is very good for your self-confidence.

Personal Balance

In reality, the pure masculine energy and the pure feminine energy are just pure fictions, which would have absolutely nothing in common if they were ever to meet each other like two different people on the street. They would, however, be extremely good complements to each other if this meeting ever took place, which, of course it never could do in the outside world.

However this meeting takes place in every human being on Earth, because all people have the masculine and feminine energy represented in their personal energy system in a given proportion, which only in a very few cases is made up of 50% of each, which is the optimal balance.

However, this balance can be achieved with an AuraTransformation™ if you decide to receive the new aura.

If you do not have balance between your masculine and feminine energies in your own energy system, you will most often try to find that balance together with the people you surround yourself with so that you might achieve an overall balance in your relationship, for example, or in your circle of friends or workplace. A very masculine person – man or woman – will therefore primarily seek relationships with people with a mostly feminine energy and vice versa, so that the overall balance is maintained. On the other hand, a very balanced person will seek relationships with other well-balanced individuals to maintain the overall balance in their life together.

The balance between the exterior and the interior is another way of looking at the balance between the masculine and feminine, where the masculine energy corresponds to the outer part of the whole and the feminine energy corresponds to the inner core. The masculine energy therefore appears as the outer shell, the shop window and the facade in which we choose to present our inner core of pure feminine energy to the outside world. This is because the feminine energy does not have enough personal flexibility in its energy structure so that, unlike the masculine energy, it is not able to communicate a message to the world in a way that is unreservedly accepted by others.

In one way or another, the pure feminine energy always has a lot of enemies on its back due to its lack of adaptability and its often great desire to provoke those around it with some very outspoken and simplistic statements which very clearly show its lack of interest in meeting other people on their terms.

It is basically the case that the pure masculine energy wants to bring many different projects to fruition but does not always know whether it will be able to get these projects completed. By contrast, the pure feminine energy is fully aware that it will get the various projects completed. However, it does not know off-hand whether it will even bother to go ahead with these projects.

So is it a question of will and ability, where the masculine energy and sperm represents the will and the feminine energy and the egg represents the ability – two qualities that we should as far as possible try to combine in our internal energy system.

The Pure Masculine Energy

People with a predominance of masculine energy are always very inspiring to be with for a short period of time. You should not however try to have any overly long discussions with them about their personal views on things. This is because, as mentioned in connection with the sperm cell, the male energy is always keen to adapt to the environment and specifically the wants and needs of the egg, which is why you can suddenly discover that they have exactly the same views as you do, even if the conversation did not begin that way!

Masculine people are always full of the power of action but without much ballast on the personal front, unless they have other people around them to back them up in their many initiatives.

They are also experts at just doing half a job and then starting on something new somewhere else, unless the pay is good and they have someone to hold the whip over them. Then, they really make an effort, as basically they are very obedient and responsive by nature – especially to their boss if he or she has a firm hand.

People with a predominantly masculine energy are very conscious about how they appear to other people and they are good at selling any product if they have a mind to. They are especially good at selling something if they are well paid for it.

They love and crave anything new and are especially good at getting new projects started, where the emphasis is on motivating the people around them to make great efforts. Here too, it is about selling in the right way, then everyone else will have to get their hands out of their pockets and work.

They are strongly characterized by changeability and are unfortunately unable to maintain stable situations for extended periods of time, so that a settled relationship and an unchanging job can quickly turn out to be something of a pain for them. They get terribly bored if they have to keep doing the same old things and restlessness is very common among people with a predominance of masculine energy.

Regarding mood, they can go straight from being genuinely happy to being extremely angry if they are having one of 'those' days. However, if the situation requires a very specific type of behaviour, they can easily deliver this in their best acting style but only for a relatively short time because as we already know, they are changeability itself.

The pure masculine energy person is a big charmer and the big seller that can fully adapt to the needs of either partner or client. However, they do not give much thought as to whether they can live up to the expectations of those around them in the longer term, whether it is a stable and permanent relationship or delivery of the desired product, as tomorrow there will be a completely new situation to adapt to.

In a relationship, their loved one may well have to compete with the masculine person's friends, favourite sport, family and job in order to get a more permanent kind of attention from their partner. The masculine person can often get into deep water in one way or another, since with the best intent they commit to everyone and therefore are often overbooked.

In a sense you could say that there is never enough time in a masculine person's life, if they are expected to meet all of their many expectations, so time keeping and boundary setting are not something that masculine people excel at.

Everything is just so busy in their daily lives, so even though they clearly have the will to want to do a whole lot, they also lack the ability and the overview to have good organizational skills. Consequently, it is a good idea to initiate a relationship with a well-balanced person who masters both the masculine and feminine energies, rather than choosing someone with predominance of just one energy.

Here are various examples briefly describing the behaviour of pure masculine energy in different situations but since there are no people with 100% pure masculine energy, these really are just examples:

Masculine people are most appreciative of sweet, well-behaved children with fixed meal and bed times and believe that children are in no way harmed by being cared for in an institution or by strangers. If the children get food, drink, sleep and warmth, they should therefore be fully satisfied. Of course it is always fun to hear about the children's many pranks, so long as it is not one's own children doing them.

Masculine people are clearly in favour of credit cards, which they also have a great need for in their lives with their many impulse buys. As for interior design, they follow the instructions of the design magazines to the letter and of course there are only the works of recognized artists hanging on the walls of their homes. Similarly, a lot of attention is paid to the advice of various magazines about fashion, 'real food' and dieting, etc. and if you can get the 'real' goods on offer, you will have no qualms about buying a dozen of the same thing at once, so that you will then have something for a rainy day.

In the world of masculine people there is no such thing as illness, unless in their circle it is in vogue as a topic of conversation on an equal footing with fitness or dieting. If their resistance to anything old and sick could be overcome, the masculine person would be the best nurse on Earth.

There will always be plenty of food and drink at a masculine person's party and its success will be measured largely on the number of people who get drunk and the number of hangovers afterwards.

As far as education is concerned, masculine people are unreservedly of the lighter genre and they would rather immerse themselves in a cartoon or a sex magazine than open a serious book. There are many more hairdressers and car salesman among people with a predominance of masculine energy than there are accountants or university students.

Masculine people always have perfect hair and make-up and since they are alpha people right down to their finger-tips, they can manage to look extremely fresh and seductive even on a sad Tuesday morning in the rain. When appearance is not enough, a cheeky or saucy smile can still win you over, for the art of seduction is strictly for people with pure masculine energy.

They also get turned on by other people's appearance and the 'right attitude' towards the outside world and they can be completely wowed by a delicious butt in a tight skirt or a pair of tight trousers!

Masculine people can get very stressed by the thought of all the things they have to achieve over the whole course of the day. They are often tired and irritable before they even get going with a particular job, unless they have some colleagues who can keep them company, or they themselves have set the project up and therefore can be expected to be passionate about the cause.

If they can charm their way into getting a few other people to do a whole lot of work for them, they will have no qualms about this. They will even repay the favour some other day if they can actually remember that far back.

You should not expect much emotional empathy from a masculine person, unless they are trying to connect with you as a possible new partner. They will then be full to the brim with understanding and so forth, all of which will be totally forgotten as soon as the partner has been snared.

When that happens, there will be many other people around who they will use their powers on instead, at work, with friends or elsewhere However, if you want for sex or a night on the town, all you have to do as a partner is just announce this to the masculine party as it will be delivered in a second. After all, those are things that are easy and do not require any great emotional empathy and understanding.

As a leader, the masculine personality is often good friends with their employees, which can sometimes diminish respect for them. Then we just open another bottle of champagne and everyone is on board again. Maybe with the exception of those who have too much feminine energy but then they are so boring that it's almost painful – at least when seen through masculine eyes.

On the sporting front, masculine people are keen on team sports where you can drink a beer in each other's company both before and after the match.

They are very competitive and are happy taking the lead in the squad if things go well, though they are also excellent at hiding in the flock if things go badly. They are real cowards who have difficulty taking responsibility, unless they can share it with others. If they can put all the blame on someone else, they are happy to do that.

The same applies to traffic. Because they love cars, racing and speed, they love to drive really fast on the roads but only if everyone else is doing the same.

If they catch the scent of a police car, however, they will immediately slow down, so that one of the other petrol heads can get the speeding fine instead. Of course, a masculine person would never speak publicly about their great love of speed, as it is not necessarily socially acceptable.

The Pure Feminine Energy

People with a predominance of feminine energy are undoubtedly very interesting both to talk to and to argue with, if you can go the distance. Many feminine people are extremely knowledgeable and insightful in their respective disciplines. On the other hand, in person they can be unusually confrontational and very outspoken in their opinions, which often seems uninspiring or even directly offensive to the people around them.

Feminine people are generally very quiet, thoughtful and introverted by nature and due to these personal qualities they can live completely isolated without any input from the wider world for long periods of time. They create their own little safe universe for themselves at home, based on their own thoughts and any ideology or belief, which reveals that they often have no real concern for anyone other than themselves. Why have a family and other people around you if you can get by so well on your own? Quite often they are just in the way and create unnecessary disturbances in your life, so you are better off by having only yourself to think about.

Feminine people mostly look inwards into their own consciousness in order to have good experiences in the form of meditation, day-dreams or memories from the past rather than seeking adventures in the outside world along with other people. If they do choose the company of other people in their lives for long or short periods, this is done solely in order to have some very specific and unique experiences with the people concerned and as soon as the experience has been gathered, the other people cease to exist for them.

Pure feminine people are extremely conscious about what they want from certain situations and from other people and they are by nature extremely cynical.

The pure feminine energy possesses great oversight but there is a strong tendency towards inaction regarding big decisions. Even though they are really good at holding together various forces, employees and family members by pulling the strings behind the scenes, they lack some of the spontaneous touch that the pure masculine energy in abundance. They can also stay with the same people, conditions and things for hundreds of years in order to stay safe. This is a personal characteristic that can be a bit reminiscent of good old-fashioned stability but actually comes nearer to being mentally and emotionally stiff and inflexible to a degree that rarely leads to anything positive for any of the parties involved.

People with a predominance of feminine energy are often very stubborn, firm in their convictions and steadfast to the last. You must therefore be extremely persistent to find just a small opening in their outer protective armour, where you can get through to their inner world and gradually influence them into thinking something other than what they have always believed and probably still believe today. Since in every feminine person there is a very good inner detective, they will probably find any loopholes and close them forever – they would never want to make the same mistake again, as it would be a real sign of weakness for the feminine person.

As in the chapter on the pure masculine energy, here are various examples, which briefly describe the behaviour of the pure feminine energy in various everyday situations. Since there are no people with 100% pure feminine energy, these are just examples:

Many feminine people have children only very late in life, as they want to be confident that they really have a

deep desire to have children at all.

Changing diapers and making baby food is not really the favourite way of spending the time for people with feminine energy but now that they have children they will obviously have the best physical, mental and emotional care they can possibly get. The children will thus be stimulated right from early childhood in terms of psychological and human care and support and unlike the children of masculine parents they will be allowed to fully express their own personalities, so long as it does not clash with their parents' views.

The parents will want to be a part of the things out in the community that have great influence on their children's daily life, for example in schools and institutions, where they will often end up sitting on the governing board.

Feminine people are usually good at both saving money and saving up and they are very choosy on the few occasions when they do go shopping. They may well have a Ferrari or an older classic car in the driveway which just stays there for weeks without being driven, as they just love to go and stroke and admire their 'beauty'.

They do not have quite the same taste as everyone else but their taste is very personal and quite different from that of their neighbours. This applies equally to interior design, art and clothing, where they are very good at creating their own style. They like order and are perfectionists in their own way but only when they have found a suitable place in the home for all of their possessions. Until then, there can be a lot of mess in their houses and they do not clean up just because guests are coming to visit but only for themselves.

Feminine people will only accept illness from the point of view of research and they often do not have time to accommodate sick people in their lives either by visiting them or having them in their thoughts. Not even if they become ill themselves. However, if someone is suddenly at death's door, whether it be a friend, acquaintance, colleague, neighbour or a family member, they will immediately rush to the patient's bedside and everything else becomes totally unimportant. This creates the basis for a really intense revisiting of the past and all the memories shared with the dying person.

Feminine people are generally very conscious of their daily diet and a product's vitamin and mineral content is carefully checked out before it finds its way into their shopping cart.

Quality comes first with regard to fresh ingredients, wine, coffee and fine chocolate, etc. and much greater emphasis is placed on enjoyment rather than productivity. It does not matter if a meal that took ten hours to prepare is consumed in less than half an hour, so long as the taste experience is unique.

Feminine people rarely invite their family or friends to a party but for a coffee instead, because they are not fans of wild parties where the guests are swinging from the chandeliers. Instead they prefer smaller events around a specific theme, where the entertainment is cultivated or distinctive and where the programme is organized in advance. The guests will be people who each have their own interesting background and the food and wine will be served in moderate portions so that nobody gets constipation or goes home drunk.

People with a predominance of feminine energy are

definitely up for a very long education where they can immerse themselves in a lot of learning and thick books. Sometimes they may be just like a walking encyclopaedia, or more like computers than flesh and blood.

Feminine people are beta-people who can sit up and work half the night and they are much more aware of their inner glow than their outer advantages.

In their relationships they have much more focus on what it means to have a shared sense of belonging and a good mutual friendship rather than on having a stimulating sex life. Emotionally they are very controlling and jealous and once they allow you in from the cold, it is almost impossible to get exit permission again.

However, if they really decide to be shameless or get up to no good, they will not be afraid of appearing naked in the middle of the street. If something really has to be done, it has of course to be done properly so that everyone can see!

Feminine people are usually very responsible in their daily lives if they have taken on a job or a task. If the pure feminine person has time on their hands and especially at work, then they will think that everyone is in the same boat – especially their partner or friends, who may suddenly receive unexpected calls from them and just be expected to talk. The concept of time is something that feminine people have a very relaxed attitude towards, as long as it applies to themselves. However, if it is another person who comes late, has to change an appointment, or uses time on the phone, they are not so accepting, unless the change creates unexpected space for something good for them.

Feminine people are not always so good at putting words to their feelings, which is why you may need to look them deeply in the eyes to read their current state of mind. Closeness and togetherness is a question of trust, where each time one is expected to surrender a little bit extra.

The pure feminine energy loves special and unique moments of all kinds, also with regard to sex, which is why it suddenly does not seem at all difficult for the person to give themselves completely if such a moment arrives. Any partner should not automatically expect complete openness from them the next time they meet, unless a new unique moment is coming.

As a leader, the feminine person likes to keep a suitable distance from their many employees and they rely on authority, power and knowledge to motivate staff to do their best work. Nobody is successful without hard work and one of the underlying objectives is clearly to get the employees to dance to the boss's tune.

With regard to sports, feminine people are primarily interested in individual performances, where they can think about things rather than just run fast and sweat. Often they are not interested in physical performance and sport at all.

Acceptable sports seen through feminine eyes are golf, chess and sometimes cycling but also car rallies, where the car does the hard work for you, as these kinds of activities can be controlled mentally.

Masculine and Feminine after an AuraTransformation™

If you have been very masculine and outgoing by nature before your AuraTransformation™, you can adjust to becoming more restrained and subdued in your attitude after it, with a greater inner calm. Not that you have to give up your masculine energy totally, as the AuraTransformation™ has the precise aim of uniting the masculine and feminine characteristics. So your being is supplemented with more feminine qualities, so that it is also possible to master these aspects of your personality in a natural way.

People who were initially very feminine and closed by nature can suddenly see themselves as being more outgoing and friendly to other people than they used to be, which usually is the reason that they wanted to be aura-transformed. For very feminine people find it infinitely difficult to meet the world if they do not get some masculine and immediate energy connected up to all their feminine energy, which the AuraTransformation™ helps them to do.

How do I keep the Balance?

You do not need to do anything special to preserve your personal balance after an AuraTransformation™ other than being true to yourself, which can be difficult for some people. If you get the urge to try to deceive yourself one last time by deliberately choosing to ignore the warning signs in a given situation, you can be pretty sure that there will be a very rapid reaction. There will be consequences and they will strike faster than lightning in the form of either physical symptoms, or of extraordinary resistance from the outside world to your work, family or daily life.

The answer as to how to preserve your personal balance intact after the AuraTransformation™ is as simple as it possibly could be: **just be honest with yourself at all times**. This should also apply to circumstances and people that are not what you would like them to be and where you might just have to put up with things for a while before they get resolved.

Knowing that things could actually be better than they are at present usually helps someone to move through any difficult situation and to get on with life.

Ways to Help your Children
and Yourself

As parents of Indigo and Crystal children, you are sometimes totally powerless when there are problems regarding the children. Here follows a few effective pieces of advice on what you can do if the need arises.

Close contact and touch is the most important thing for Indigo and Crystal children and you will always get the best result by giving your child a big hug if the child has personal problems, discomfort or real pain somewhere.

Hold the child to your heart and try to transfer peace to him or her in that way. It is however a prerequisite that you have peace inside yourself, otherwise you should get someone else to hold the child. This can also help you and other adults with either the new or old aura structure to find inner peace.

If your child is restless and is feeling bad, you may want to massage the child's forehead and temples lightly with small circular movements to create a calming and soporific effect.

Above all, make sure to give your child a strong feeling that you will always be there for them, no matter what happens. This method can also help you and other adults with either the new or old aura structure to relax better.

If your Indigo child becomes restless for no apparent reason, you can use your thoughts to surround the child with indigo/violet colour or energy. This corresponds to the Indigo child's own basic energy in the aura, so the child will quickly feel comfortable in the energy and become calm.

This is especially good if your child has trouble falling asleep. This method can also be used with good effect on Indigo adults.

If your Crystal child becomes restless for no apparent reason, you can use your thoughts to surround the child with a transparent crystalline violet colour or energy with pink undertones and then the child will calm down immediately. This colour combination corresponds to the child's own basic energy in the aura. This method can also be used on adult Crystal people.

If you want to protect your child during the day when the child is in school or day care, etc. and you are not in direct contact with the child, you can focus your thoughts into thinking that the child *is now optimally protected by the energy directly from the highest cosmic force.*

You could possibly say it loud for yourself or repeat the words several times in your head. In this way you help your child to be surrounded by an extra strong protective membrane of very high-frequency energy, which at the consciousness level burns away all negativity from around the child.

This will also help your child to avoid bad experiences during the day. Daily life will of course still go on as usual, so they can still learn from the things that they are experiencing on their path but thanks to the protection the risk of the child getting hurt is greatly diminished, unless the child has actually deserved it in some way.

You can also use these protective words on yourself or on others you care a lot about.

If your child begins to imitate negative characteristics of their peers, or begins to frequent anti-social elements in society, you can use your thoughts to draw all your child's personal energies back from the people who are using their bad influence on them.

Then send all the other peoples' negative energies that your child has mistakenly attracted back to the people themselves, so that your child can be normalized as quickly as possible on the consciousness level.

Immediately after this you will have a far greater chance of having a good, sensible talk with your child about the situation than would otherwise have been impossible. The effect is greatest if you repeat the afore-mentioned procedure as often as possible. The method can also be used in relation to yourself and other people, where the people around you have a bad influence on your life and often it will be quickly confirmed that it is well worth you spending time drawing your personal energies back to you and sending other people's energies back to them, which will motivate you to continue.

If your child feels low in energy or unstable after having been with other people who may have unknowingly drawn energy from the child, you can use your thoughts to draw all your child's personal energies back from these people.

Then send all the other peoples' energies that your child mistakenly attracted without even knowing it back to the people themselves.

This method can also be used on yourself and other adults.

The methods described are not limited to work only in those contexts. They can also be used in other similar situations.

If you want to get to know some more energy balancing methods, I recommend you read my husband's and my two little and easy to read books *"The Little Energy Guide 1"* and *"Get Your Power Back Now!"*.

The New Aura
– from the Spiritual Perspective

The Transition to the New Time

The New Time energy represents such a strong spiritual power that it is not easy for everyone to change their energy system so that it can handle the new high energy love frequencies.

This is like imagining putting the inner workings of a modern-day computer inside the shell of a computer from 1980! The difference between then and now is simply too big for the two things to work together properly, which is why God had the foresight to allow people to make their own choice to change or not.

An old hard drive can of course still work well in the casing of similar age for the rest of its lifespan, in the same way that older people and people with very established attitudes to life can easily maintain their soul aura, although its functionality and capacity compared to the new aura will clearly be slightly or more decidedly reduced.

With the new aura, you get your own free will to do as you wish in any situation, unless you deliberately want others to decide for you.

However, it is expected that with regard to realizing your personal mission in life you should collaborate with the higher powers in working towards getting planet Earth to act as a harmonious unit.

On the spirit level, the focus is on balance, while on the soul level it has nearly always been the custom to channel energy in the form of pure light. The light corresponds to only one half of the balance energy which the New Time energy consists of, which is why darkness may have to be involved in all energy work in the future and on an equal footing with the light in order achieve total balance in line with the New Time energy.

You should not however, get involved in working specifically with dark energy without light being involved as well, which is why it is of course best to work with clean balance energy without using just one side of the equation.

There is great versatility associated with working with balance rather than solely working with light. So to be able to change the various unsatisfactory situations around the world, you should preferably be able to address the issue from two angles – both from inside and from outside and also in a 'nice' and in a less nice way – which is why it is a definite advantage to be familiar with the energy of both light and dark energy and the procedure to tackle any possible problems. This is not in order to be rude and boundary-crossing with other people but rather so that you are able to cope well with the people who use this kind of behaviour. Especially if this behaviour is being used against you.

We can imagine that the best police officer is often the one who can best understand the criminal's mind without being a criminal himself.

If you want to help others to get a better life it is clearly an advantage to have tried things on your own body, so you know right down to your marrow what you have to deal with in the concrete situation. Then you also know how to talk to people to get them to listen in a proper manner and possibly to move in a new and positive direction.

One must know all the pitfalls from yourself and your own life to get into contact with others who find themselves in a hole right now.

It is perfectly natural therefore that a former alcoholic or drug addict is the best person to help other alcoholics or addicts with their life because they are not perceived as an enemy but rather as a friend in need and living proof that there is a way out of the mess.

They have already been through the mill themselves, so they know the darkness from the inside and are therefore able to come through with some positive messages to the addicts in a way which would never be accepted if it came from a therapist who had only read about these things.

For there are not many people who like people who preach or are lacking an inner understanding of how things hang together. This is something you probably should think about if you have a desire to go out into the world to help or influence other people in a particular direction.

The same applies if you want to talk on behalf of a good cause. You should be careful not to preach your message to the people around you, as they will quickly close up inside at the thought that here comes someone who wants to make themselves look clever at your expense.

The simple message of the New Time energy is therefore that there must be balance in the way we approach the world, so nobody gets knocked over by others or risks having to drag a full load on their own while other people stand by and watch. Everyone should bring something to the whole, so that there can be an overall integrated wholeness with many different equal opportunities to benefit a lot of people.

The Spiritual World

To be able to master the New Time energy and get a good return from your new aura it is by no means necessary to have any knowledge of consciousness and the underlying spiritual dimension. However, to get a good return from this chapter it is necessary that you have an inner understanding that consciousness represents the invisible substance that gives life to our human bodies. People who have nothing to live for on either the inner or the outer level in their life find it very hard to stay alive for very long if their physical body is seriously weakened.

If the spark of life is therefore reduced in the individual person, the spirit and consciousness slowly disappear from the body and if the spark of life completely disappears, the spirit disappears from the body forever, leaving only the heart and other vital organs to keep the physical body going. It is thus consciousness that keeps us alive inside from an energy point of view.

At the same time, consciousness corresponds to the aura and radiance that we are all surrounded by just outside the body. The aura and radiance represent a force field of fine vibrating energy that each of us surrounds ourselves with to some degree. This force field allows your fellow humans to read information about you from afar without you having to answer a lot of personal questions. It is always possible for the people around you to see many things on the subconscious level, so they know in advance whether you are interesting to them as a person or not. The aura, consciousness and radiance, or whatever we choose to call it, makes it possible to spot at a distance good or bad chemistry between people, so that they can avoid any disappointment when they get to know each other.

As we have seen, the main aim of being aura-transformed is that you get your intuition and spiritual energy directly connected to your body so that body and spirit can work freely together. But what exactly is happening on the spiritual level when the AuraTransformation™ takes place, since you will suddenly be able to capture relevant information for the benefit of both yourself and others?

Who sits and pulls the strings behind the scenes and how does this overall spiritual management fit in with having your own completely free will?

In response to these questions, here is a simplified insight into the structure of Earth's spiritual hinterland which for many non-spiritually interested people may sound like complete nonsense but which for others, represents the pure truth.

Earth's Spiritual Hinterland

Most people know the story of Adam and Eve and Paradise and have heard various stories from Nordic, Roman and Greek mythology, etc., or have heard about Jesus' suffering on the cross, all of which are accounts of very spiritual people who have physically existed here on Earth in times past. However, the spiritual world has rarely been particularly strongly manifested on the planet at once, in the sense that not many great spiritual masters and archangels have previously been incarnated on Earth at the same time.

For example, Jesus naturally lived at the same time as his mother, Archangel Mary but he first came across other true believers, people with a very high spiritual consciousness like John, Mark, Matthew, Paul, Peter and Luke and others at an adult age, when he went out and preached the Christian gospel.

They did not then have the status of spiritual master like Jesus but they were on the way to attaining it.

Behind the curtain, the Earth's spiritual hinterland has been guided for countless millennia by a hierarchy consisting of some very spiritually conscious masters and archangels with God sitting at the top of the pyramid. These very spiritually conscious beings have all maintained control of consciousness in the Earth's population through the concepts of obedience to authority and karma, which have guided all human thought and behaviour, as well as deciding what type of development it has been useful to send to Earth at any given time.

The spiritual system has been built up like a pyramid in which all the less enlightened souls have found themselves at the bottom of the pyramid, where there has been a blockage in the struggle to progress further up the hierarchical system. These are the souls which throughout time were born as 'ordinary people' around the Earth.

Similarly there have been some more aware souls with a larger spiritual capacity further up the hierarchy who have been born here on Earth throughout the ages and at the unconscious level they have had a stronger memory than the afore-mentioned ordinary people' concerning their spiritual affiliation to Earth's consciousness hinterland.

Of all these souls and spiritual beings, it is the masters and archangels at the top of the pyramid who have had the best conditions to understand the connection between the visible Earth and its spiritual hinterland but as previously stated, they have never all been incarnated on Earth at the same time. They have therefore had a whole host of spiritually equal beings to draw general knowledge and awareness from the Earth's spiritual hinterland when the need for this has arisen in connection with their current earthly lives which have not always been particularly exciting. For it can be extremely difficult for a very high and finely vibrating spiritual being to find a life purpose in the Earth's often heavy energies, unless they have the ability to make a living as an artist or a philosopher, which is not always easy on this planet.

Their personal force has been that in the area of consciousness, they have known the true way to God's power, so they have found it easier to find strength in themselves than has been possible for so many other people with a less spiritual consciousness.

Through the many millennia in which the spiritual hierarchy that we are all part of on this planet has been looking after the Earth's consciousness hinterland, people have been guided through their predetermined and karma-driven lives to gradually make more human effort, for example in relation to their beliefs and lifestyles and in relation to the whole. In this way they have been able to gain a greater spiritual insight and a better position in the spiritual hierarchy behind the scenes, both in actual life and also when they leave it. However, there are only very few people who have really been able to feel God's power when their consciousness has been followed from above on their path through life.

Instead many people have been tortured or killed in the name of faith, where the killers have then completely rejected any responsibility as they believed they were guided from above.

The biggest and hardest task for the Earth's spiritual hinterland has been to guide the Earth's physical population via karma-control and intuition etc. to live a better life in harmony with each other and with the whole. It cannot be said to have been a complete success. There have therefore had to be some new and different energy initiatives in the Earth's consciousness hinterland to increase the speed of development and accountability in the population and this is how the New Time energy and the new aura and the concept of AuraTransformation™ have come into the picture. With an AuraTransformation™ you move out into the spirit level with your consciousness rather than being located on the soul level where you can only be dictated to from above without even being able to question or assess the accuracy of the information you receive.

Out on the spirit level, which since 1987 the whole of the soul-driven hierarchy of Earth's consciousness hinterland has slowly moved out onto, everyone is responsible for their own actions. The hammer will fall perfectly naturally on those who have single-handedly carried out ugly deeds no matter where they have been guided from. They can just say no thanks and not perform the task.

The same quick direct payment model will also apply to people's good behaviour and positive efforts, where the rewards will come comparably quickly.

The spiritual hinterland thus ensures that all living people are continuously equipped with the best intentions for themselves and for the whole through various intuitive influences from above, or from good advice coming from people's everyday environment. However, it is always up to each person through their own free will to make the final choice and carry out the actions here on Earth, which is why it is they themselves who will quickly get rewarded or penalised for this.

If you have problems with your intuition, an AuraTransformation™ may help. With the spirit body connected directly to the physical body, Earth's spiritual hinterland has much better opportunities for intuitively influencing the individual to move in a favourable direction, which is to the benefit of both the person themselves and the whole. Most people are seldom really happy inside if things are just going well for them and they are not going correspondingly well for the people around them, which is why there also must be balance in this area between the individual and the community.

It will surprise no-one that there will always be different views on things, whether you have the old or the new aura, since there are no two people on this Earth – regardless of nationality, gender and skin colour – who think alike. So there can be many disagreements between people. People can have bad chemistry and you may be forced to accept this about yourself. If people, especially adults, disagree, they must also be big enough to accept the consequences of this and keep a distance from each other instead of constantly provoking a fight. After all, every day, an entire generation of children are mirroring their parents and other adults, as well as their sometimes unfortunate behaviour and if you do not watch out, when they eventually become adults, these children will simply repeat the behaviour of their parents and other adults without even thinking about why they are doing it, until one day they meet other adults who behave in a more balanced way.

As far back as the origin of the Earth it has been understood that the planet's population should find an internal balance between people, communities and countries, where respect and openness towards different ways of thinking and new ways of doing things prevail but at present there is obviously a long way to go before this goal is reached.

Many people will fight for their own beliefs, which they will be allowed to do for a little while longer, so long as they do not involve innocent people and expose them to danger but they must also be prepared to accept the consequences of their actions, if one of their own family members, friends or neighbours falls in the heat of battle, for instance. Also in the interests of the people around them they have to seek outlying locations on Earth to fight their battles, such as in the mountainous regions of Afghanistan or other similar places, which has already started to happen regularly.

Also, in the future, many troublemakers and agitators from very different nationalities will disappear in large numbers from the surface of the Earth, as they kill themselves and each other in their many internal conflicts and struggles – especially religious ones – which Earth's spiritual hinterland views with deep scepticism.

Light and Dark

Here on Earth, due to the concept of karma and the soul influx, people have always dichotomised everything into light and dark, where light has stood for everything that is good and contained the message of love, while darkness has represented the satanic and pure evil. These energies have been reflected in various ways in people's behaviour and nature and in relation to the concepts of faith and justice.

According to the general living instructions from the soul-driven hierarchical hinterland, certain things have been absolutely right and other things have been completely wrong and that is just the way it has been.

> The exclusively spirit-related New Time energy is more nuanced, so in the future, many new values and ways of living will arise intuitively and in people's consciousness with the help of the Earth's spiritual hinterland. These values will all be related to the realization and achievement of the concept of balance in all areas of human life.

There will no longer be the dichotomy of light and dark, two separate and contradictory entities, which is how many people had previously experienced the energies and also how many alternative practitioners have seen things. Many therapists have sought the light and tried to eliminate the darkness in people's consciousness, which often leads to people being easily fooled and naive at a higher level as well as having a strong tendency for the people who only practice light work in their everyday lives to close their eyes to the real world.

Darkness should not be eliminated completely, as the two extreme and opposing energies – light and darkness – each contribute to the whole picture here on Earth.

The light provides a sharpness of perception and image in experiences of all kinds and in life in general, while the dark correspondingly creates depth in perception, images and life.

So the New Time energy basically consists of an overall balance between light and darkness, which in future will be more and more integrated in earthly and human contexts.

Creating Balance

Spiritually aware people should not believe they can make the world a better place just by thinking positive thoughts and meditating. These days there is a need for action and a great deal of will to create balance in life. Similarly, very physical people with their feet firmly on the ground will now think more about life and be equipped with some degree of knowledge of consciousness connections, thus gaining a more holistic view of themselves and of life in general. This is certainly one of the intentions behind the 'Project Balance' for Earth, where, in the future, the light and dark, spiritual and earthly energies will work hand in hand in all human contexts.

We must also learn to ask each other for advice when we have problems and not judge the people around us so much on the basis of who we may believe has the right answer to a given question. Sometimes you can really be quite surprised where help is to be found, because you may not have previously thought that this person or these people had such knowledge or personal resources.

The fact is that a very large number of the spiritual masters and archangels, such as Jesus, Mother Mary and the Archangel Michael and so on, who the Earth's population has always turned to through the prayers they have daily sent to heaven, are today alive and well and living as relatively ordinary people somewhere on the planet. Maybe your neighbour or your best friend is one of those with great spiritual entities, who are so well camouflaged that you cannot see or feel it clearly about them.

There are therefore, a great many 'Angels in Disguise' on Earth at this time to help and influence different people at close proximity, as the countless influences and intuitive thoughts from the spiritual hinterland cannot do it alone.

God's Power

Many people can therefore benefit greatly from listening to the common sense that the people around them often come up with every day, because in reality, there can be a much greater truth about life hidden behind very ordinary words than you might expect. Of course, not everyone is lucky enough to have access to a helpful angel or a spiritual master in disguise on a daily basis.

If you want to get good advice or an answer to a question from the Earth's spiritual hinterland and there is no-one immediately in your social circle who can come up with any really wise words, you can decide to send your request directly to the top, where God's power is found. This may take the form of a prayer or of your directing your thoughts directly towards God's power. Since God's power is always the highest possible energy capacity, it is probably also the best at delegating out tasks to the right hands, both here on Earth and in heaven. And who knows, maybe it will suddenly be your neighbour that comes up with the redemptive words as God's power has made sure that it has a hand in things behind the scenes.

After an AuraTransformation™ it is especially recommended that you send your prayers directly to God's power, rather than sending them in the direction of various masters and archangels on the spiritual level. Very often your personal energy capacity will be so great that you might just as well ask yourself for an answer instead of asking a spiritual master and if you know that you do not know the answer, then there is probably only God's power to turn to to get it.

On the spirit level, the various masters and archangels also directly address God's power to get help if they do not know the answer.

Spirit Mates

In the New Time, all human beings have the chance to find true love in the form of their spirit mate, who is the person with whom they emerged together energetically on the spirit level right back at the origin of existence. This is a very intense and affirmative experience on all levels, which in future will lead to many lasting relationship connections that will be impossible to break due to the feeling of cohesion both internally and externally.

Spirit mates are people who are simultaneously each other's mirror images and opposite poles and who cannot fail to be both physically and spiritually attracted to each other. It can however be a big emotional mouthful to relate to seeing your own reflection in another person – most often of the opposite sex – as most relationships in the old soul-related world have only been based on people being attracted to their opposite, which the spirit mate also represents in the New Time energy.

Therefore, many soul mates risk losing a little of their personal shine in comparison with the new spirit mates, when they emerge from the mists at some point.

You can read more about Spirit Mates in my husband's and my book *"Spirit Mates – The New Time Relationship"*.

Master in your own House – Free Will

Many people often have a strong feeling that fate has a hand in their choice of partner and often this feeling or belief is reinforced in a strange way by the fact that both partners have the same feeling of having known each other before and in some cases forever.

Most of us can quickly agree that there is much more between heaven and Earth than we humans can understand and explain or can at all accommodate with our everyday waking consciousness. It is therefore not so unlikely that we have all lived many times before, either here on Earth or some other place out in the vastness of the universe. In any event, some of us know each other from somewhere else, which our subconscious periodically tries to make us aware of through various déjà vu experiences with other people we know in everyday life. If you believe in reincarnation, where humans and animals are constantly reborn in a new body and in a new place on Earth, it would seem that the same people follow each other in groups down through their respective lives. However, the individuals in the group do not always take the same roles in relation to each other from one life to the next. The person who was your mother in a past life might easily be your sister or cousin or a really good friend in this one.

The concepts of fate and karma are phenomena that will disappear forever when you have an AuraTransformation™, as consciousness leaves the soul level to instead enter the spiritual energy on the Indigo or Crystal level. With the new aura you will instead make your own fortune, with the possibility of choosing the framework for your future life. In return there will be much more focus on your life purpose and dharma, where the ultimate goal of your life is determined from birth but where all the people with the new aura will be free to choose their own paths to fulfilling and realizing their respective life purposes.

Becoming karma-free on the soul level and master in their own house on the spirit level thus increases people's awareness and responsibility, so that they can contribute to creating their own life in accordance with modern life premises, with the ability to continuously learn from life while they are living it.

Adults of the Future

Future Crystal people are able to think holistically and individually at the same time.

They think both about the family and society as a whole and they function as a fully integrated part of any whole while also thinking about their own well-being and having full focus on themselves as individuals.

In 2012 and 2013, the Crystal energy finally arrived on the Earth in its most updated form but how will society actually develop from 2012 onwards with all the new Indigo adults at the helm?

The pure Indigo children, who are born from 1995 and subsequent years, will be the first adults with the New Time energy, which on the energetic level will have direct influence on society from around 2020 and onwards. By then there will be a large number of adults around the globe who have had the pure Indigo energy completely integrated into their aura structure through some form of consciousness expansion.

After this it will take another 17-20 years before the pure Crystal children grow up and become influential in society worldwide and at that time there will also be a large number of adults who have had their Indigo energy upgraded to Crystal energy.

All Crystal adults who in the period up to 2012-13 were lucky enough to get their proper energy affiliation made visible to both themselves and others will become more and more satisfied in life.

Already by 2012 these people will have had a really strong feeling of playing on home ground, so even though right now it may seem like there will be a very long time before the Crystal energy emerges fully into the different communities on Earth, that moment is not actually that far away.

All the new Indigo and Crystal children, through their ways of being, opinions and personal needs, will always help shape the development of society in a direction that will best meet their human needs in the future. There are also always trendsetters in business and in society generally who are able to anticipate and comprehend the needs of future generations long before parents manage to do so for their children's needs.

In society, nothing big happens from one day to the next. So there will need to be a natural and smooth transition from the existing form of society, based on the old time soul energy, through the Indigo energy and beyond to the total impact of the pure Crystal energy on all societies around the world. This is an influence on society which will be significantly different from the many widely different forms of governance around the world today, where not everyone is able to cooperate with everyone else. In the future, there will probably exist many different types of communities around the world but the communities will always have overall cooperation with each other for the benefit of Earth as a whole.

Future Crystal Adults

Here follows a brief review of the factors, which I have already touched on, that have significance for future Crystal people, when one fine day they enter adult life. The same factors apply, to a less comprehensive degree, to future Indigo adults:

Future Crystal adults will be very aware of how they educate and influence their children in everyday life and as a relic from the period around the year 2000, in the future there will be many mixed families consisting of your, my and our jointly grown children, who may now have children of their own. So there will be many people gathered around the dinner table in homes around the world, even if it is only the immediate family who has gathered.

This in no way excludes the existence of the company of good friends at the same dinner table as it is precisely spirit-fellowship that will bring people to gather in large groups in the future.

Future parents will be very direct in their parenting but as soon as the basic messages are stored on the children's hard drives, a far more creative influence will be launched to inspire children to learn more. The same methods will apply in schools, daycare centers and care facilities worldwide, to ensure that each child's ethical, compassionate and professional foundation is so stable that it can be securely built upon.

Children need a good, stable foundation in life so that they can develop positively. It is thus beneficial that all 'irregularities' in connection with the individual child's attitude and behaviour are eliminated at as early an age as possible in order to avoid enormous damage to humanity and society in the future.

Since all Crystal children are fast-paced and very clear and strong by nature, they are extremely quick to find different ways of doing things even at a very early age and here all negative imprinting will influence children just as much as positive imprinting does, if it is the only imprinting children receive from their parents and the people around them. Children are, however, quick to erase all negative imprinting as soon as they begin to exclusively receive positive imprinting.

It will not benefit Crystal children to believe that they can do a whole lot more than they actually can. Parents should spend the time it takes to get children to understand what resources and rights they have at their current age, so that there will not be future misunderstandings in connection with the child's self-image.

> Crystal people pay a lot of attention to prevention if it is possible to do so and they feel that it is appropriate but they are also good at healing once the damage is done.

In future, Crystal parents will ensure that their children receive individual imprinting in all common areas where there is a need for it but they will also ensure that their children can cope positively in a large community of the family, daycare center, school or after-school club. Later the children will be able to cope as both young people and adults in the workplace, in their own family and in society generally, where the demands for independence and inner and outer harmony will be increased significantly compared with today.

Future Crystal adults are very aware of who they are and what human and professional qualifications they possess and they are actually not selfish individuals as some of today's adults erroneously think.

Future Crystal people have a very clear attitude to themselves, to others and to society as a whole and they are completely aware of their own position in life. For example, they do not lie to themselves that they are bigger, better, smaller or worse in some contexts than they are. They know who they are and where they stand as a person in any context and are extremely realistic in their views on all personal and social relationships.

They are very conscious and consistent regarding their own choices in life with regard to family, friends, jobs, hobbies, etc. They know who they want to have a close relationship with and who they do not want to be close to in daily life and they lay all their cards on the table in their dealings with everybody. No-one who has a relationship with an individual Crystal person is ever in doubt about who they are as a person and what they stand for. Otherwise you just have to ask and you will get an answer.

Crystal people look into the future for their 'real' partner the first time. They do not mistakenly have several 'wrong' relationships during their quest for the real one just because they cannot bear to be alone or to get a lot of experiences just for the sake of experience. They prioritize and select much more strictly in their life than today's adults do and they do not like to compromise in any situation whatsoever.

Because of their very pure style, they can easily figure out how to stick to the rules if they need to and to not use foul play against their opponents.

Crystal people cannot easily be encouraged to do stupid things just because other people with lower frequency energy than theirs try to provoke them into it. They speak frankly about things and choose how they want to relate to specific people and situations in the future, where the solution can easily be that the Crystal person and their opponents choose to totally avoid each other.

In the future, balance and harmony in a meaningful everyday life, as well as justice, will have great significance to all Crystal people in all areas of life, both in leisure and work.

For instance, in business they will demand that there is an overall coherence and direct correlation between the company's and their own basic philosophy and attitudes to life. Otherwise they will feel no loyalty to their workplace at all.

The Crystal person must be able to relate positively to the company's overall goals and also to the milestones relating to them directly. Otherwise the job will be meaningless to them, as they need to engage fully with what they are doing.

It is also important that things in daily life function in the workplace in relation to the various practical, human and economic aspects and that there is fairness, balance and harmony between the Crystal person's own efforts in the company and the payment that the person receives for their efforts. All Crystal people are extremely conscious that they must give something in order to get something back and that they are expected to give extra if the company decides to invest heavily in developing their professional knowledge and/or personal qualifications.

The Crystal person needs to feel a sense of freedom at work and they need to be able to work in their own way and from their own assumptions, which of course, is something that should be discussed when they are hired so that both employer and employee are clear about what they can expect from each other. This is a trust that Crystal people expect and which they honour to the full. Since Crystal people are individualists with a strong focus on the whole, they never behave selfishly in business or in society in general. In a work context, they will always think about the whole but at the same time, they will also be very aware of where they themselves, their boss, colleagues and/or customers are to be found in this whole.

Last but not least, Crystal people should be able to see an ongoing development in their company, their team and their own individual growth in order to be able to maintain strong personal commitment and so they will want above all to have some personal influence in relation to their job.

Crystal people will in general like to have influence everywhere in society where they have a personal interest, which may cover everything from politics, environmental and social conditions, the improvement of living conditions for children, the elderly and disabled people, changes of local plans in the community or the fight for a new football pitch in the children's playground, etc.

In future, personal involvement will be much higher for everyone than it has ever been on this planet, because most people will have a specific life purpose which involves people other than just themselves.

Crystal people have come to Earth to make a major positive difference in all earthly matters. They therefore deal promptly with any injustices that they themselves or their nearest and dearest encounter at home, at school, in the daycare center, at work, or in society in general.

Crystal people will not stand for injustice of any kind and act rapidly and constructively to resolve matters.

Action follows thought absolutely unconditionally in the lives of all Crystal people.

Conclusion

Some years ago I received an email from an Aura Mediator™ whom I had trained myself. The email made me think a lot about how important it is in life to put things and energies together as perfectly as is possible as if we do not, things can turn from being heavenly to being hell on Earth!

Heaven is where:
The police are British,
The cooks French,
The mechanics German,
The lovers Italian,
And it's all organized by the Swiss.

Hell is where:
The cooks are British,
The mechanics French,
The lovers Swiss,
The police German,
And it's all organized by the Italians.

Of course there are good English cooks, as recently European television has been swarming with them but at the time I received the email there were not many Danes who were particularly flattering about English food, except, perhaps, for the English Breakfast.

So you should create the best life conditions for yourself and remember to always let other people live their lives as they wish, unless this has a direct adverse impact on you or on others.
    There are things and situations on this Earth which have never been acceptable, nor ever will be and so of course you should not just sit and smile if people try to violate your boundaries or

those of the people close to you .

My advice to you is to be as certain as possible to create clarity in your own life and to sort the sheep from the goats on a daily basis, so that you know what you are dealing with and can act accordingly.

That way, you will not end up by punching your best friend and kissing your enemy.

Warm greetings,
Anni Sennov

The Founder of AuraTransformation™

Anni Sennov

Anni Sennov is the woman behind AuraTransformation™ and the founder of the Aura Mediator Courses™ which take place in different countries, mainly in Europe (**www.auratransforma tion.com**).

She works on a daily basis with the course instructors of the Aura Mediator Courses™ in several countries.

Anni Sennov is a clairvoyant advisor, international lecturer and the author of more than 20 books about energy, consciousness and self-development, as well as New Time children and relation-ships, several of which have been translated from Danish into a number of languages.

Together with her husband Carsten Sennov, she is a partner in the publishing company Good Adventures Publishing (**www. good-adventures.com**) and the management consulting and coaching company SennovPartners (**www.sennovpartners. com**), where she is a consultant in the fields of personal develop-ment, energy and consciousness.

Anni and Carsten Sennov have developed the personality type indicator the four element profile™ (**www.fourelement profile.eu**), that consists of four main energies corresponding to the four elements of Fire, Water, Earth and Air, which are each present in everyone in a variety of combinations of balance and strength. Multiple courses are offered on how to understand and integrate these elements both for private people as well as businesses.

Anni Sennov was born in Denmark in 1962 and originally began her career in the financial world. Since 1993 she has had her own practice of personal counselling and her great strength is her ability to clairvoyantly perceive multiple relevant circumstances pertaining to her clients' personality and consciousness.

Anni Sennov's work and books are mentioned in numerous magazines, newspapers and have featured on radio and television in many countries, both in and outside of Europe.

You can connect to Anni Sennov's profile on LinkedIn, Google+, Twitter and Facebook, where she has an English author profile:

facebook.com/pages/Anni-Sennov/141606735859411

You can follow her blog and subscribe to her English newsletter at **www.annisennov.com**.

Furthermore, you can subscribe to the English four element profile™ newsletter at **www.fourelementprofile.eu**.

Last but not least, you can watch videos about AuraTransformation™ at **www.youtube.com/sennovpartners** and about the four element profile™ at **www.youtube.com/fourelement profile**.

Anni Sennov's Authorship

Current books:

Balance on All Levels with the Crystal and Indigo Energies (English)
Balance på alle planer med krystal- & indigoenergien (Danish)
Kristalli- ja indigoenergiat ja kokonaisvaltainen tasapaino (Finnish)
Les Énergies Cristal et Indigo : un équilibre à tous les niveaux (French)
Balanse på alle plan med krystall- og indigoenergien (Norwegian)
Balans på alla plan med kristall- och indigoenergin (Swedish)

The Crystal Human and the Crystallization Process Part I (English)
The Crystal Human and the Crystallization Process Part II (English)
Krystalmennesket & Krystalliseringsprocessen (Danish)
Kristallmänniskan och Kristalliseringsprocessen (Swedish)

Golden Age, Golden Earth (English)
Den Gyldne Jord (Danish)
Jordens Gyllene Tid (Swedish)

Karma-free in the New Time (English)
Karmasta vapaana uuteen aikakauteen (Finnish)
Karmafri i den nye tiden (Norwegian)
Karmafri i den nya tiden (Swedish)

Spirit Mates - The New Time Relationship - Co-author: Carsten Sennov (English)
Henkikumppanuus – uuden aikakauden suhde (Finnish)
Spirit Mates – The New Time Relationship (Japanese)
Andedualitet - Den Nya Tidens förhållande (Swedish)

Get Your Power Back Now! - Co-author: Carsten Sennov (English)
Tag din kraft tilbage nu! (Danish)
Astu omaan voimaasi! (Finnish)
Récupère ton pouvoir maintenant! (French)
Energy of the Art of Self-defense (Japanese) *(2-in-1: The Little Energy Guide 1 + Get Your Power Back Now!)*

Ta tilbake kraften din nå! (Norwegian)
Ta tillbaka din kraft nu! (Swedish)

The Little Energy Guide 1 - Co-author: Carsten Sennov (English)
Malý energetický průvodce 1 (Czech)
Den lille energiguide 1 (Danish)
Väike energia teejuht 1 (Estonian)
Pieni energiaopas 1 (Finnish)
Le petit guide de l'énergie 1 (French)
Energy of the Art of Self-defense (Japanese) *(2-in-1: The Little Energy Guide 1 + Get Your Power Back Now!)*
Den lille energiguiden 1 (Norwegian)
Мини-руководство по работе с энергией, часть 1 (Russian)
Den lilla energiguiden 1 (Swedish)

Crystal Children, Indigo Children and Adults of the Future (English)
Kristall-lapsed, indigolapsed ja uue ajastu täiskasvanud (Estonian)
Pure Indigo & Pure Crystal Children (Japanese)
Кристальные дети,дети Индигои взрослые нового времени (Russian)
Kristallbarn, indigobarn och framtidens vuxna (Swedish)

Love, Sex and Attraction - A Short Guide to a Successful Relationship (English)

(Be a Conscious Leader in your own Life)
Bliv bevidst leder i dit eget liv (Danish) - Co-author: Carsten Sennov
Bli medveten Ledare i ditt eget liv (Swedish)

Sold out titles can be found at www.annisennov.com.

Related books

The Crystal Human and the Crystallization Process Part I and Part II
by Anni Sennov

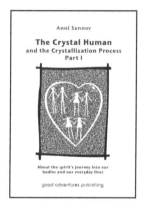
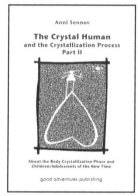

Get Your Power Back Now!
by Anni & Carsten Sennov

Spirit Mates
The New Time Relationship
by Anni & Carsten Sennov

See Barnes & Noble, Amazon and others

The Aura Mediator Courses™

The Aura Mediator Course is a 5-day intensive course whereby the participants obtain all the abilities and experience necessary to successfully perform AuraTransformation treatments.

Who can take the course?

- People with a passion and sensitivity for working with themselves, with other individuals and/or with society at large through a development and expansion of consciousness and awareness stand-point

- Those who wish to enhance their own abilities, life skills and overall quality of life

- People who wish to help others by synchronizing and updating their energy fields with the rapidly changing energies of our time

- People who wish to use their skills with Aura-Transformation™ as an add-on to their already established business, or as the main focus of what they offer to clients

All participants are required to have had an AuraTransformation™ at least 2 months prior to the course.

What happens during the Aura Mediator Course?

This course is an intensive process which is experienced both theoretically, as well as within one's own physical body and aura. The work with AuraTransformation™ and therefore the Aura Mediator Course, deals with integrating and balancing the new aspects of the four elements (Fire, Water, Earth and Air) as a part of the crystallizing process where one integrates the spirit into the aura and all the way into the physical body.

One gets a thorough understanding of working with balance, frequencies and how to maintain one's own energy sovereignty as well as how to work with different characteristic types of clients.

The first part of the course is an individual consultation lasting 3½-4 hours. The course participant's individual Crystal life purpose will begin to unfold more clearly from this process. One's Crystal source and potential as an Aura Mediator™ will be opened and activated as a preparation for part 2, the practical and theoretical part of the course.

The second part of the course is held in small groups of 4 to 8 participants with the course instructor and an assistant if the group is large. There will be a dynamic and interactive passage through the theoretical sections of the course material. There will also be hands-on experience working professionally with clients under direct supervision from the course instructor.

Following the initial 5-day intensive course there will be a 2-month support phase by phone and email for questions and advice regarding work with AuraTransformation™ clients.

Registration

See current courses and sign up for the Aura Mediator Course at **www.auratransformation.com**.